Praise for
How to Fight Racism

"In *How to Fight Racism Young Readers Edition*, Jemar Tisby provides a much-needed resource to help young people understand the injustice of racism, how to identify signs of racism, and how to practically fight against racism. This book will help you to discover how you can be the change you want to see in this world."

Christine Caine, founder A21 & Propel Women

"*How to Fight Racism Young Reader's Edition* is an honest but refreshing look at the ugly aspects of American history that have divided us, but it also gives us the themes that unite us. Dr. Tisby takes time to not only give history, he includes encouraging stories of those from the past who've bravely united us."

BJ Thompson, executive director of Build A Better Us

"In a world constantly asking us to choose 'biblical principles' over 'wokeness,' *How to Fight Racism Young Reader's Edition* reminds us the very measure of faith in action is how it responds to the word's injustices. This book offers language, tools, framing, and important historical perspective not often taught in schools. It is a must read for today's students and tomorrow's leaders."

Nelba Marquez-Green, licensed marriage and family therapist
and founder of This Grieving Life and the Ana Grace Project

"Jemar Tisby has created essential reading for any young person asking, 'Yeah, but what can *I* do?' In a compelling way, he invites us around his table—a table big enough for all of our questions, curiosities, and fears—and guides us with vivid storytelling and practical steps. As a parent, I'm thrilled for this resource in the continual work of bending our universe toward understanding, equity, and justice."

Bethany Anne Lind, actor in *Ozark*, *Doom Patrol*, *Reprisal*, and *Stranger Things*

"Our children need to learn the truth about the history of race in America. This powerful book will inspire young minds to pursue compassion, knowledge, and the necessary work of racial justice in their lives of faith."

Kate Bowler, Duke professor and *New York Times* bestselling author of *Everything Happens for a Reason (and Other Lies I've Loved)* and *Blessed: A History of the American Prosperity Gospel*

Also by Jemar Tisby

FOR ADULTS

The Color of Compromise

How to Fight Racism

YOUNG READER'S EDITION

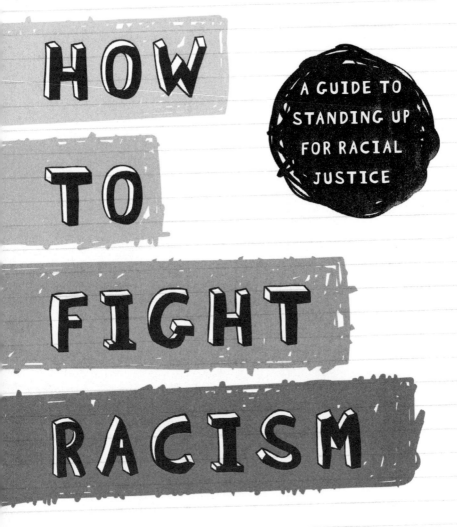

HOW TO FIGHT RACISM

A GUIDE TO STANDING UP FOR RACIAL JUSTICE

JEMAR TISBY

with Josh Mosey

ZONDER**kidz**

To my daughters: choose the right
side and fight hard. —J.M.

———————

ZONDERKIDZ

How to Fight Racism Young Reader's Edition
Copyright © 2022 by Jemar Tisby

Requests for information should be addressed to:
Zonderkidz, *3900 Sparks Dr. SE, Grand Rapids, Michigan 49546*

ISBN 978-0-310-75104-5 (hardcover)
ISBN 978-0-310-75126-7 (audio download)
ISBN 978-0-310-75124-3 (ebook)

Cover Design: Brand Navigation
Interior Design: Denise Froehlich

Printed in the United States of America

———————

22 23 24 25 26 / LSC / 10 9 8 7 6 5 4 3 2 1

Contents

PART 2: RELATIONSHIPS

PART 3: COMMITMENT

CHAPTER 1

How to Fight Racism

Growing up, I went to a Catholic elementary school, even though I wasn't Catholic. And in fifth grade, I played basketball, even though I was a terrible basketball player. But I lived just outside of Chicago in the 1990s when the Bulls basketball team was on their NBA championship winning streak and Michael Jordan was on his way to becoming the G.O.A.T. (Greatest Of All Time).

I mean, I wasn't that into sports compared to my friends, but I definitely had this life-size poster of Jordan (6 feet 6 inches tall) that I got from some car dealership, where you could stand next to it and see how you measured up. I was short. Still am. But back then, everyone wanted to be like Mike.

And if you were Black like I was (and still am), there was this expectation that you were good at basketball. But me? In fifth grade, I was always the last one off the bench. The other kid who was my same height, only white instead of Black, was the second-to-last one off the bench.

At the time, I thought it was embarrassing. Black kids are supposed to be good at basketball, but here's this white kid who's the same size I am, and he's better than I am. I felt like I was somehow not Black enough, like I was failing my race or whatever. But mixed in with that was this feeling like, "Why should people expect me to be good just because I'm Black?"

Before I unpack that, however, let me tell you about where I grew up—Waukegan, Illinois. Waukegan is about a forty-five-minute drive from downtown Chicago. It's a working-class kind of town on the harbor where people made things with their hands, then sent them off somewhere else by boat. The part of town I lived in was full of Black and brown people, mostly Latino. I remember that all the signs downtown were in Spanish, and a lot of the guys I hung out with spoke at least a bit of Spanish, but a lot of them spoke it fluently. Today, some people act like Latino folks are a threat, that immigration is a big scary deal, but back when I was in fifth grade, I thought it was cool that these kids who were my age could speak two languages when I could only speak one.

My dad moved our family to Waukegan just before I was born. He worked at a company that made medicine, managing a team from his cubicle. As far as I know, he was the first of his family to go to college and get an office job like that. All the other people who worked with my dad and did what he did lived in Chicago's middle-class suburbs, which were mostly white. But my dad made the intentional choice to move farther away from his job to a city where none of his coworkers lived because there were more people of color in Waukegan than in other places. It was a poorer area. People from my dad's work would invite him over to their houses, but nobody wanted to come to our house because it was in the "dangerous" town.

I think he wanted to raise his family in a community like the one he grew up in. My parents grew up in Michigan, in a segregated neighborhood. It wasn't like they could have lived anywhere else when they were kids. Back then, there were rules that said Black people weren't allowed to live next to white people. But I remember my dad talking about how that neighborhood was his whole world, how there was a real sense of community and togetherness there. There were doctors and lawyers and teachers and custodians and plumbers, all Black, all side by side, all supporting each other as best they could. So when he got his cubicle job, he moved us to Waukegan, which was mostly brown and Black people like his neighborhood in Michigan, and life was good.

But back to basketball, which I wasn't good at, and going to a Catholic school, even though I wasn't Catholic. The mix of kids in my school looked just like the rest of the population from working-class Waukegan. About half of the kids were Latino, about 20 percent were Black, another 20 percent were white, and the rest were a mix of East Asian and other folks. When I was on the fifth-grade basketball team, our gym was so old that the floor had all these dents and chips in it, and it had been waxed a million different times and was uneven. We didn't even have locker rooms. All the boys would have to go into this big custodial closet kind of thing to change clothes. And it was fine because it was all we knew.

It was fine until we started traveling to play basketball against the other Catholic schools in the area. I'll always remember visiting this one school in another Chicago suburb where most of the people were white, a place my family could have lived because of my dad's job. We walked in, and their gym had this brand-new rubber floor. I didn't even know you could have floors made of rubber! And it was huge! It had all these nice things, like actual locker rooms and snazzy logos painted on the wall. It even seemed brighter because all the lights worked and the ceiling was like a mile high.

At that moment, I remember thinking, *This isn't fair. Just because our school is full of Black and brown kids and this school is full of white kids, why do they have all the nice stuff and we have all the broken-down stuff?*

Where to Begin

There's a reason you are reading this book. Maybe you're going to read it with your family. Maybe you're in a class and your teacher wants you to understand why the fight against racism is important. Maybe you've noticed the contrast between the gym at your school and the gym from the school across town, where the people look different from you. Maybe you've seen news stories you don't understand because they use terms like **anti-Black police brutality** and **white supremacy** and **racial profiling**. (I'll do my best to explain terms like these in the boxes on the page where they show up, but if you still don't understand them, you can always ask a grown-up too.) Maybe you already know what those things are and you're just looking for what you need to do next.

Anti-Black police brutality: Police methods that treat Black people in more forceful, and sometimes dangerous, ways compared to how officers treat white people

White supremacy: A system of power where language, lifestyles, and values held by white people are considered normal and better than those held by people of color

Racial profiling: Paying closer attention to Black people and people of color because you suspect them of illegal activity based on the color of their skin alone

Whatever your reason for reading, my hope is that you'll come away with a better understanding of where we've been as a nation, a deeper knowledge of who you are as a person, a vibrant connection to people of all backgrounds, and a stronger sense of purpose to fix what needs to be fixed in our broken world.

Because our world *is* broken. Racism is just one of the ways the brokenness comes through. What is racism exactly? I like the definition Beverly Daniel Tatum reaches in her book *Why Are All the Black Kids Sitting Together in the Cafeteria? And Other Conversations About Race*: racism is a system of oppression based on race.[1]

Let's break that down a bit. A system is an intentionally organized way of doing something. It isn't when something

Racism is a system of oppression based on race.

randomly happens—it's *making* something happen. For example, the public school system was built in a certain way so students would have teachers who report to principals, who report to a superintendent, who reports to a school board, who makes sure that a school is following the laws that were set up by the larger government. It's organized to run in a certain way.

Oppression is when one person or group of people tries to control another person or group of people. Oppression can take the form of a schoolyard bully, a mean older sibling, or anyone who puts themself in charge when they don't have a right to be in charge. In each case, the person uses their power and authority to make life harder for other people.

Race is a category you get placed in because of your skin color. Race gives certain groups unfair benefits, and other groups don't get those benefits just because they're in a different group.

---

1. This is my paraphrase of Beverly Daniel Tatum's breakdown of racism in her book, which she also based on David Wellman's definition and argument in *Portraits of White Racism* (Cambridge: Cambridge University Press, 1997), chapter 1, where he states that racism is "a system of advantage based on race."

To say that racism is a system of oppression based on race is to say that things have been organized by people in society to give undeserved authority and advantages to one group of people over another because of the color of their skin. And the sad truth is that racism causes all kinds of problems in the world. So when you say you want to fight racism, the first problem you come up against is, "Where do I start?"

Should we look first at examples of modern racism? Maybe we should start with historical racism like the transatlantic slave trade, **lynchings**, or the **Ku Klux Klan**. Should we talk about how Thomas Jefferson wrote the Declaration of Independence and said, "All men are created equal" when at the same time he enslaved Black people?

Lynching: A form of terrorism where groups of white people kill Black people who have been accused of a crime but haven't been given a fair trial in court

Ku Klux Klan: A white supremacist group that was popular after slavery ended and opposed, sometimes violently, Black people getting their rights as American citizens

The problem of racism is older than America but as current as today's headlines. It's as violent and wrong as a public lynching, but it can dress up in fine clothes to attend church on Sunday. It can seem far removed when discussed in history books, but it's as personal as being afraid of someone because they look different than you.

With a problem this big, where do you start?

With you.

Right now.

Reading this book.

Learning about racism and its history in this country as well as in your own life. Figuring out how you can make relationships with people who are different from you. Accepting the challenge to change the future.

If the fight against racism seems like a huge responsibility, that's because it is. But it isn't bigger than you can handle because you aren't fighting alone. Change can start to happen when groups of people—big or small—come together and dedicate themselves to fighting racism in all the ways it shows up in the world. And history shows us, and hope needs us to believe, that when people work together, they can find creative solutions to society's biggest problems.

This fight isn't just for grown-ups. Some of the greatest advances in the fight against racism have happened because kids fight too.

The Birmingham Children's Crusade of 1963

During the Civil Rights era of the 1950s and 1960s, Birmingham, Alabama, was an example of racism in action. **Segregation** in the city made it so Black people were not allowed in certain businesses and only allowed to go to others on "colored days."

> **Segregation**: A system of keeping Black people and other people of color separated from white people

In his famous "Letter from Birmingham Jail," Dr. Martin Luther King Jr. said, "Birmingham is probably the most thoroughly segregated city in the United States. Its ugly record of brutality is widely known. Negroes have experienced grossly unjust treatment in the court. There have been more unsolved bombings of Negro homes and churches in Birmingham than in any other city in the nation."

Civil rights groups, including King's Southern Christian Leadership Conference (SCLC), planned a series of nonviolent protests to convince Birmingham's leaders to **desegregate** the city. Things got worse when a circuit court judge allowed

Desegregate: To remove the rules that keep white people and Black people apart so everyone can have equal access to the same resources

Boycott: Agree as a community not to buy or use services from a specific business as a form of protest against the business's unfair rules or policies

the police to arrest people who protested, demonstrated, or **boycotted** certain businesses in town.

When the arrests of thousands of adults did little to change people's minds, SCLC leader James Bevel started planning a "Children's Crusade."

Throughout April 1963, thousands of kids were trained in nonviolent tactics. On May 2, those kids gathered at 16th Street Baptist Church before heading into the city to peacefully protest segregation. By that evening, almost one thousand of those kids were arrested.

The youngest protester to be arrested was Audrey Faye Hendricks, age nine. Audrey's family was already involved in the Civil Rights movement.

"Well for me, there was no way not to be involved," said Audrey in an interview with PBS years later. "My parents were involved from the point that I could remember. My mother was the assistant secretary of the Alabama Christian Movement. My father had gone to jail for riding on the bus. My church was involved. There was just no way around it."[2]

After one Civil Rights mass meeting, Audrey told her parents she wanted to participate in the protests, knowing she would go to jail. Her parents agreed to let her.

Audrey spent a week in juvenile hall at the Birmingham City Jail. She wasn't allowed to see her family. She had no clean clothes to change into. She didn't even have a toothbrush. The only blessing of being arrested the first day of the

---

2. https://pbslearningmedia.org/resource/iml04.soc.ush.civil.ahendric/audrey-hendricks/.

crusade was that she was already behind bars when the racist commissioner of public safety, Bull Connor, ordered police officers to spray kids with powerful water hoses, hit them with batons, and threaten them with police dogs.

In spite of these new dangers, children continued their nonviolent demonstrations over the next few days. By this time, photographers from major news companies were being sent to Birmingham to record the police brutality. These photos and videos were broadcast around the country and led to a national outcry. Birmingham business owners started feeling the pressure to change.

On May 10, just over a week after the Children's Crusade began, city leaders reached an agreement with Civil Rights leaders to desegregate their businesses and free everyone who had been jailed during the protests.

Birmingham's racist history didn't stop with the end of the crusade, but the crusade was the thing that helped convince President John F. Kennedy to pass new Civil Rights laws that could be enforced by the military. In June 1963, he told the nation that the racism happening in Birmingham and elsewhere could no longer be ignored.

In 1964, after President Kennedy was killed, the Civil Rights Act became law in America, making it illegal to **discriminate** on the basis of race, color, religion, sex, or national origin.

Can kids actually fight against racism?

Audrey Faye Hendricks did.

> **Discriminate**: To treat people differently based on characteristics such as how they look, where they're from, or what they believe

The thousands of others who stood with her against fire hoses, dogs, and the policemen's batons did.

You can too.

Questions to Consider

- How would you define racism in your own words?
- What is something you would be willing to go to jail for, like Audrey Faye Hendricks did?

CHAPTER 2

The ARC of Racial Justice

Racism uses lots of different ways to lie to people, to make them feel like less than they are, and to make them seem less than human. It's like a football playbook that has all the plays the other team is going to use to win. As people working for racial justice, we need to get to know this playbook so we can be ready for anything racism throws at us.

This book is structured around a model I created called the ARC of Racial Justice. ARC is an acronym that stands for awareness, relationships, and commitment. It's a way to understand how to fight racism with our heads, hands, and hearts.

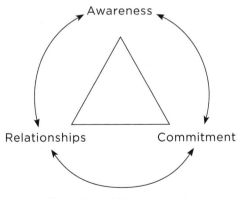

The ARC of Racial Justice

Understanding racism's playbook is where awareness comes in. It is the facts, knowledge, and information required to fight racism. It's the "head" portion of the head-hands-heart trio, and these three all depend on each other to work. In this book, you will discover ways to increase your awareness by studying history, exploring your own story of race, and understanding what God says about the built-in worth of the human person.

All racial justice is relational. What sparks the desire for people to see change? How does someone develop their feeling of responsibility to combat racism? Often it comes through relationships with other people who actually experience racist words and actions.

Think of relationships as the tender heart of racial justice. You can't pursue racial justice without real, authentic relationships with people who are different from you. For example, if you are white, saying, "I have a friend who is Black" is a good start, but that friendship alone isn't enough. How close are you to that friend? How much do you know about their life? Do you share things with each other? That is what matters when we talk about relationships in this book.

Besides building awareness and developing relationships, what truly makes big changes on the racial justice front is a commitment to take apart racist structures, laws, and policies. What does that mean? Well, because racism has been a problem in our world for so long, it has twisted and tangled many parts of society to the point it doesn't work fairly for all people.

Did you know that there used to be laws in different cities that were created to make all the Black people live in poorer parts of town? The amount of money a school has to pay teachers and fix buildings depends on how much money the people in that community have. Which means the poorer parts of town—the parts where Black people were forced to live—couldn't afford to pay teachers a good salary or keep their buildings repaired. Richer areas of town—where white people were allowed to live—were able to provide better educational experiences for their kids. Although the unfair laws that forced Black people into poorer areas have changed, people who come from poorer areas still have a tougher time moving out of those neighborhoods than those from wealthier areas. In order to set things right so all people have equal access to things like quality schools, it will take a commitment on everyone's part to fix the unfair rules that create so many problems.

To actually change society—to set right the historic wrongs that made things like racial segregation in public schools possible—people must commit to changing how society works. The rules have to be rewritten so they lead to greater **equity** among people of all races and ethnicities.[1]

Think of commitment as the "hands" aspect of the head-hands-heart metaphor.

The ARC of Racial Justice is an easier way to think of the bigger picture of racial progress. Many of us naturally

Equity: Giving everyone what they need to succeed, even if what they need is different from what others need

lean toward one area of this fight. Maybe you love to devour books and information about race to increase your knowledge.

---

1. Throughout this book I often use the term *equity* rather than *equality*. The Lakeshore Ethnic Diversity Alliance website explains the difference this way: "Equality aims to promote fairness. This is only effective if all participants have similar starting points and the same access to resources for achieving their desired goals. This approach can intentionally disregard the needs of individuals. Equity on the other hand demands that individual needs are taken into consideration. It accounts for identities (race, ethnicity, ability, nationality, gender, etc.) and circumstances that may otherwise hinder the success of one participant over another." See "What's the Difference between 'Equity' and 'Equality'?," Lakeshore Ethnic Diversity Alliance, https://ethnicdiversity.org/equity-vs-equality/.

Perhaps you are great at making relationships with people from different backgrounds and experiences. Or you might already be active on the front lines, taking part in campaigns for radical change. These are all admirable steps, but the best approach to racial justice includes all three aspects: awareness, relationships, and commitment.

That isn't to say that awareness, relationships, and commitment need to exist in perfect balance. Sometimes, your awareness of racism will grow quickly because of a new relationship, but you won't know what to do about what you've seen or heard. At other times, you'll find a way to commit to an anti-racist cause, but you won't have many relationships with people of other races.

The ARC of Racial Justice doesn't always move forward in a straight line. In other words, you won't move directly from awareness to relationships to commitment. Rather, you will grow in each part of the ARC at the same time. Sometimes one part will help you make progress in the other areas.

The process of growing in awareness, relationships, and commitment never ends. You will always be learning, you will always be developing relationships, and you will always be discovering new ways to commit to a life of racial justice.

Standing Up for Racial Justice

The subtitle of this book is "A Guide to Standing Up for Racial Justice." To stand up for something means defending it because it's under attack. Racial justice has been under attack since before the United States even started. And although progress has been made since the days of the transatlantic slave trade, we haven't arrived at a racially just world yet.

In 1963, Audrey Faye Hendricks stood up for her right to be treated like an equal. She was only nine years old when she marched with thousands of other kids in the Birmingham Children's Crusade. She understood the situation because she had experienced injustice. She had relationships with others in the community who felt the same way. She was committed to changing society, even though she knew she would be arrested for peacefully demonstrating.

Standing up doesn't mean standing still. Racial justice is a journey. The progress may be slower than you'd like, and you might make mistakes along the way, but we don't quit just because the path is long and hard.

The destination is racial equity and justice for people of every racial and ethnic background. The endpoint is harmony, where unity wins, even when people are very different. But this is a trip that lasts your whole life. Seeing racial justice as a journey encourages us to think about fighting racism as an ongoing series of steps instead of walking toward a finish line. Instead of defining success by the results we achieve, we should define it by the actions we take.

As we begin to treat each other with more love, as we are able to see life from different perspectives, it will not only change the world around us; it will also change *us*. As I have taken steps to promote racial justice, I have developed more endurance, discovered untapped wells of creativity, and experienced more joy than I ever expected. This journey can change you too, if you let it.

As you venture into unknown territory, it is important to realize the journey looks different for everyone. No one has the same starting point, nor are we all moving at the same pace. Black people and people of color have been fighting racism our whole lives.[2] We have thought about racism, prayed about it, cried about it, written about it, marched against it, and resisted it as the very means of our survival.

This is not new to us.

At the same time, we still have more to learn, and we can always get better at pursuing justice. For some white people, this may be a brand-new discussion.

As a young person, you are naturally nearer the starting point than the end. Reading this book is a great first step on your journey. You may stumble on the way, but everyone learns to walk one step at a time. It means strengthening your leg muscles through practice. It means getting back up when you fall.

Standing up for racial justice; dancing the steps of awareness, relationships, and commitment; venturing out on the journey: all of these ways of thinking about race will help us move beyond easy definitions of racist and not racist. In reality, no one has a perfect record when it comes to racism.

People of color who believe the stereotypes about themselves may act in prejudiced ways toward white people or toward other racial and ethnic minorities. White people may support the racist status quo—current way of doing things—by choosing comfort and privilege over the fights and change that racial justice requires.

At times, even the most closed-minded person may stumble into words or actions that promote equity. But since you know that everyone's journey is different, your challenge is to focus

---

2. Throughout the book I often use the phrase "Black people and other people of color." Distinguishing between these groups highlights the unique experience of Black people in the United States due to the existence of race-based chattel slavery. A similar distinction can be made for the particular histories of colonization that Native Americans and other indigenous groups have faced. This language does not imply that any group deserves more sympathy for the suffering they endured, just that histories of oppression differ between people groups.

on your own quest, your own dance, your own ability to stand up for racial justice.

Courageous Christianity

While this book is meant for any young person ready to start their journey toward racial justice, we'll be working together from a specifically Christian perspective. I am convinced that Christianity must be included in the fight against racism for several reasons.

First, Christians must fight racism as a matter of responding to the past. And unfortunately, throughout the history of the United States (and around the world), people who said they were Christians acted in some very racist ways.

As a small example, close your eyes and picture the face of Jesus. For many of us, we have to force ourselves to picture Jesus as a brown-skinned Jewish man from Nazareth instead of the European-looking image of Jesus with flowing auburn hair, thin lips, and blue eyes. Visual representations of Jesus as a white man are ways of saying who Christianity is meant for. When Jesus was pictured as a white man instead of a person of color (which he definitely was), the message was sent out that Jesus came primarily for the good of white people.

But people who said they were Christians were also guilty of worse things than painting Jesus the wrong color. Some supported slavery. You might wonder how this could be possible since slavery is so obviously wrong, but some Christians believed **race-based chattel slavery** and racial segregation were what God wanted.

Even though we know today

Race-based chattel slavery: The practice of owning Black people for their labor and treating them as though they were property that could be bought and sold and used like an object these things are not what God wanted, since Christians haven't always been on the right side of the racial justice debate (and sadly, some still aren't), there is good reason for Christians to be the ones to set things right.

Second, Christianity gives us understandable reasons for why racial justice is important. In modern times, most people agree that treating other people fairly and not using race as an excuse for inequality are good ideas. But why are these things good? What is it about human beings that means we should treat one another as equals? Where do these ideas come from?

Christianity teaches that all people are made in the image of God. The people who claimed to be Christians in the times of slavery and segregation lost sight of God's image in people who looked different from them.

Third, Christianity has within it the resources to rebel against racism and white supremacy. Time and again, Christianity has provided courage for activists fighting for racial justice. Ida B. Wells, Prathia Hall, Rosa Parks, and many other fighters for racial justice movements counted on their Christian faith to give them courage to fight against racism.

Courageous Christianity contrasts with the false version of Christianity that led so many religious people to cooperate with racism instead of challenging it. In "Letter from Birmingham Jail," Martin Luther King Jr. wrote, "All too many [religious people] have been more cautious than courageous and have remained silent behind the anesthetizing security of stained-glass windows."

Have you ever had a body part "fall asleep"? If you sit cross-legged for a long time, you may lose feeling in one or both feet. You can poke it with your finger, but you don't feel anything because your foot has gone numb. When you switch up the way you are sitting, you start to get that pins-and-needles sensation as your foot gets feeling back. It isn't a comfortable feeling, but unless you go through the pins-and-needles, you won't be able to stand up and walk forward.

What Martin Luther King Jr. meant in his letter is that too many Christians have had their sense of racial justice fall asleep. They're numb to the problems around them because they don't see them or maybe don't want to see them. Courageous Christianity requires us to go through the pins-and-needles moment, no matter how uncomfortable it is, so we can take a stand and walk forward in the confidence that comes with faith in God.

It is time for the church to wake up and bring racial justice to all the places injustice is found, and to spread the love of God that inspires its people to act on behalf of their neighbors. Courageous Christianity dares to love through action and to risk everything for the sake of justice.

An Exercise in Prophetic Imagination

The book you are reading right now is an exercise in "prophetic imagination."

In the Old Testament, prophets like Elijah and Isaiah and Jeremiah were responsible for telling the kings and leaders of their day what God wanted them to do. These prophets saw the wrong choices their leaders were making, but they also imagined how things could be different if the leaders listened to God.

Many adults have limits on their ability to imagine that things could be different, because they are so used to how things have been for such a long time. But you, as a young person, can imagine how things could be in the future. By spending time exploring strategies for change, you may be inspired to create new ways to fix issues of racism.

This book is an invitation to dream. It is an open door for you to explore the possibilities of a world in which racism does not define so much of our reality, an opportunity to reimagine a life where we acknowledge our differences but do not use them to dismiss or dehumanize others.

People of any race or ethnicity will find helpful suggestions and ideas in the chapters that follow. The dynamics—the forces at work within a system—of race affect people across the color spectrum. What is helpful for taking apart anti-Asian racism, for instance, will probably work in fighting anti-Black racism as well. While most of the examples apply specifically to Black-white racial dynamics, the things you'll read could apply to the prejudice that other groups experience as well.

I believe it will be most helpful to read this book with other people. It could be a friend, a church group, or your family. Processing the history and ideas in these pages will be more fruitful when you can hear other perspectives. As you consider what actions you should take, start by choosing one or two specific actions from each chapter. You may want to pick the practices that seem easily achievable first, then do others that feel like a stretch, and then a few that may strike you as truly radical.

Above all, don't worry too much about where to begin. Just start somewhere. If you want a complete step-by-step plan for racial justice before you get involved, you will remain stuck in place. Often throughout history, people became activists because they took a single action.

A Word to Black Kids and Kids of Color

Even though racism is not something invented by Black people or other people of color, we still have a responsibility to fight racism. White people are the ones who benefit, in some ways, from racism. So white people have a lot of responsibility to fight racism. But Black people and other people of color are the ones who know best how dangerous racism is.

It's like if a bully always hangs out at the same corner in your neighborhood. Maybe you had to find out the hard way that the bully is only looking to hurt people. But now that you know, you can warn other people, and you can even tell the bully why their actions are so harmful because you've felt them!

That being said, you need to take care of yourself. I am a Black person myself, and I know from experience how exhausting racism can be. There's always another comment, always another insult, always another injustice. The world does not *give* us breaks from racism, so we have to *take* our rest. Fighting racism is a lifelong journey. But just like in a long race, you have to pace yourself.

Take time out to unplug from the fight against racism regularly. Find out what gives you energy and joy and do that. It could be going for a walk outside, spending time with friends, writing poems or songs, or turning off your tablet or smartphone just to cut off the endless flow of information.

Yes, as Black people and people of color we need to be in this fight against racism. But don't let racism run you into the ground. You've got a lot to offer the world. We need you.

There eventually comes a moment when a person decides that doing nothing is more costly than doing something.

Maybe you've already had that moment, which is why you are reading this book. Maybe reading this book will lead to that moment for you.

We need another generation of people willing to fight for freedom. We need a movement of people who will not back away in the face of racist evils. If you are willing to be part of this movement, and if you want to better equip yourself for the struggle, then read this book and take the next step on the journey toward racial justice.

Questions to Consider

- Which part of the ARC of Racial Justice do you think you are strongest in?
- Think of someone you know who took a stand for something. What did they do? How did it work out?
- Why is it important for Christians to be courageous, especially when it comes to issues of racial injustice?

PART 1:
AWARENESS

Emmett's Fight

Emmett Till was born in Chicago on July 25, 1941. He was raised by his exceptional mom, Mamie Till, on Chicago's South Side in a neighborhood filled with Black-owned businesses. Although his mom had gone to a mostly white high school—and had excelled there—Emmett attended the segregated McCosh Grammar School. There, he made a lot of friends and was known for his sense of humor.

It wasn't always about making people laugh though. With his mom working twelve-hour days as a clerk for the air force, Emmett proved to be responsible with housework. His mother once recalled, "He told me if I would work, and make money, he would take care of everything else. He cleaned, and he cooked quite a bit. And he even took over the laundry."[1]

At the time, Chicago wasn't a very safe place for Black people to be. As Black families moved out of the South after the end of slavery, tensions rose in the cities where they settled. In the 1910s and 1920s, the number of Black Chicagoans more than doubled. The new residents came because the city offered jobs and opportunities. It was even the home of the largest

---

1. From the Emmitt Till Legacy Foundation, "Emmitt's Story," https://emmetttilllegacyfoundation.com/emmetts-story/.

Black newspaper, the *Chicago Defender*. But the rapid population growth was often met with violence. Between July 1917 and March 1921, the city reported fifty-eight bombings of buildings that had been rented or purchased by Blacks in white Chicago neighborhoods.

In August 1955, Emmett's great-uncle, Moses Wright, came up from Mississippi to visit family in Chicago. When he returned to the South, Wright brought Emmett and his cousin, Wheeler Parker, back with him. Fourteen-year-old Emmett even turned down an offer from his mom for some open-road driving lessons on a road trip to Omaha, Nebraska, in order to spend time with his cousins in Mississippi.

The night before Emmett left, his mother gave him a ring that belonged to his deceased father, Louis Till, marked with the initials *L.T.* The next day, she saw him off at the train station. It was the last time she saw him alive.

Three days after arriving in Money, Mississippi, where his cousins lived, Emmett and a group of teenagers went into Bryant's Grocery and Meat Market to buy some refreshments. What exactly happened inside the store may never be known. Emmett bought some bubblegum and was later accused of either whistling at, talking to, or touching the hand of the store's white female clerk, Carolyn Bryant. While these accusations may not sound like a big deal today, a Black boy flirting with a white woman in any way was considered more than rude. It was thought to be an expression of animal-like behavior on the part of the boy and a stain of dishonor on the part of the woman.

Many years later, when she was in her mid-seventies, Carolyn Bryant—whose husband owned Bryant's Grocery and Meat Market—would admit that her exchange with Emmett never justified what happened next.

At two o'clock in the morning on August 28, 1955, Roy Bryant and J.W. Milam, Carolyn's husband and brother-in-law, stomped up to Moses Wright's cabin and yelled out, "This is Mr. Bryant. We're here to talk to you about that boy from Chicago, the one that done the talking up at Money."

The two white men carried pistols and smelled strongly of whiskey. Against Moses Wright's protests, Bryant and Milam found Emmett in bed in the back room and kidnapped him. The men beat Emmett severely, shot him, then strung barbed wire and a seventy-five-pound metal fan to his body, and dumped him in the Tallahatchie River.

Moses Wright reported Emmett's disappearance to the authorities, and three days later, his body was found by a fisherman. Because of the violence he endured, the only way they knew it was Emmett was because of the ring on his finger, engraved with his father's initials.

The court trial against Roy Bryant and J.W. Milam began on September 19, 1955. Although Moses Wright took the witness stand and identified the two men as Emmett's kidnappers and killers—putting his own life at risk for testifying against them—the panel of all-white, all-male jurors declared Bryant and Milam to be not guilty.

In later interviews, nine of the twelve jurors on the case said nothing that was said at the trial would have changed anything. They knew that Bryant and Milam had killed Emmett Till, but they would have voted not guilty anyway. They felt that white people needed to stick together because the Southern way of life would have suffered if they had voted otherwise.

In 1955, two white men getting away with the murder of a Black teen in Mississippi wouldn't have received much attention—but Emmett's mother refused to let that happen. She decided to hold an open casket funeral, where Emmett's body could be seen. While having her fourteen-year-old's mangled body on display caused Mamie Till incredible pain, she wanted to let the world see what had happened.

Photos of Emmett's body in the open casket were published in the previously mentioned *Chicago Defender* and *Jet*, a highly influential Black magazine. Before long, mainstream news organizations picked up the story.

Public attention turned to national outrage at the outcome of Emmett's murder trial. Individual organizations that were fighting for civil rights began to team up. The lack of justice around Emmett Till's death inspired a whole generation to act.

It wasn't the words Emmett said to Carolyn Bryant, the white store clerk, that led to his murder. It was Emmett's race.

Questions to Consider

- In what ways did Emmett Till embody the image of God?
- In what ways do you?

CHAPTER 3

The Science of Race

In the years before the Civil War, Dr. Samuel Morton was one of the most respected scientists in America. Morton was one of the founders of the Pennsylvania Medical College in Philadelphia and taught classes in anatomy (the study of how the body is put together) from 1839 until 1843. While some people collect rocks or books or LEGO minifigures, Dr. Samuel Morton collected human skulls.

By studying the skulls from people around the world, Morton came up with a theory that there were five basic races on the planet—Whites, East Asians, Southeast Asians, Native Americans, and Blacks—created at different times in history, and that white people were the most intelligent. Morton's claim that Black people were at the bottom of the intelligence spectrum was wholeheartedly embraced by defenders of slavery.

When Morton died in 1851, the *Charleston Medical Journal* in South Carolina praised him for "giving the negro his true position as an inferior race."

Although Morton seemed to be on the cutting edge of scientific research for his time, his findings have since been proven entirely wrong. Genetic research has shown us that the concept of "race" as it relates to skin color and other physical characteristics is a matter of social dynamics (what society decides is important), not science.

According to science, every human is from Africa if you go back in their family tree far enough. Humans with lighter skin tones have simply adapted to be able to live in places with less sunlight. Skin color is determined by the amount of and type of **melanin** in the skin.

Melanin: The pigment that gives skin and hair its color

Think of melanin like the body's natural sunscreen. People who live near the equator typically have dark skin, which is a useful shield against ultraviolet (UV) radiation. Those who live near the north or south pole have paler skin because it promotes the production of vitamin D, which we need to stay healthy. When people get too much UV radiation, they get sunburns and have an increased chance of getting skin cancer, or "melanoma," so if you live somewhere with more sun, it is useful to have naturally darker skin.

The instructions for the amount and type of melanin in a person's skin comes from that person's DNA—the body's instructions for how it is put together, what it looks like, and how it works. And 99.9 percent of our DNA is identical from one person to the next, which means we are all a lot more the same than different. Physicist Riccardo Sabatini explained that if we printed our entire genetic code on paper, it would take 262,000 pages and only about 500 of those pages would differ from person to person.[1]

Interestingly, there's more genetic diversity between the peoples of Africa than on all the other continents combined.

---

1. Riccardo Sabatini, "How to Read the Genome and Build a Human Being," Filmed February 2016, in Vancouver, British Columbia, TED video, www.ted.com/talks/riccardo _sabatini_how_to_read_the_genome_and_build_a_human_being.

That means that the DNA of a Khoe-San boy from South Africa is more different from a Turkana girl from Kenya than a white boy from Michigan is from a Han girl from China.

But none of these minor biological differences set built-in limits on intelligence, cultural creativity, or where someone fits into society. Instead, limits have been placed by one group of people over another as individuals and communities made purposeful decisions to hold up one group over others.

When Dr. Samuel Morton came up with his theories about different races, white people used his "science" to justify their position as the group in charge. Unfortunately, Morton's followers have shaped society, and just because his science has been debunked, it doesn't mean that society has changed to fit with the truth that there is only one race: the human race.

The Three Main Features of Race in America

The concept of race in the US context has three distinct features: it is elastic; based on physical features; and has social meaning, which affects a person's experience within society.

What does it mean to say the concept of race is elastic? *Elastic* means that racial groupings don't always stay the same. Definitions of who fits into which racial category change over time. There was a time in US history when the Irish might not have been considered "white," yet over the course of decades they became firmly entrenched in the racial ranking system as white people. Those who were or were not considered Black oftentimes depended on skin tone and subjective opinion rather than ancestry.

In the United States, race has largely been defined in terms of physical appearance. It tends to be viewed as something related to hair texture, body type, and nose and lip shape. But skin color remains the essential feature of race. Anyone deemed nonwhite falls outside the highest level of the racial ranking system; the darker-skinned a person, the lower their position in society. People of color have even bought into this idea of race. Among various people groups, "colorism"—a practice in which people of color discriminate among themselves based on skin color—remains a problematic issue.

White supremacy[2], of which racism is just one part, builds circles within circles where white people of European descent are in the center, the place of privilege and importance. Those in or near the center enjoy greater access to the best job opportunities, higher-quality education, more financial wealth, and the presumption of innocence and normality. Outside of this central circle are all other people of color including people of Latin American, Asian, and Native American descent. Black has been made out to be the "opposite" of white and, therefore, has always occupied the outermost circle.

No matter how much Black people try to fit in by changing the way they talk, their style of dress, and who they socialize with, blackness in a white supremacist society can always be turned against someone. This is why even when they were the President and First Lady of the United States, Barack and Michelle Obama endured racist attacks. No matter their level of achievement, people of African descent in the United States, especially those with darker skin, are always placed in the outermost ring of American social circles.

This is what a white-centered society looks like. This is

---

2. For a deeper look at the topic of white supremacy, turn to Additional Articles at the back of this book.

why for many decades, Band-Aids only came in the color beige to match the skin of people of European descent. This is why Kodak, the camera and film company, set all their colors to a photo of a white model, who was deemed "standard" or "normal," while people of other levels of darkness almost always came out under- or overexposed in developed film.

Race has been created and re-created by social forces that change over time. No person of any race or ethnicity has a biological or spiritual claim to being better than anyone else. Race has served to separate society into different levels for the benefit of a few people who have been defined as white to the misfortune of anyone considered nonwhite or "of color." Although race is something imagined (or constructed), its effects are real. From life span to salary to where you live, race has a measurable impact on a person's quality of life.

Blue Eyes & Brown Eyes

What would happen in our world if we didn't group people based on skin color but on eye color instead?

When Martin Luther King Jr. was killed in 1968, a third-grade teacher in Riceville, Iowa, named Jane Elliot knew she needed to help kids understand the significance of King's death. But how could a white teacher from a white community teach a class of white third-graders about the reality of discrimination? How could she help them understand the kind of hatred that led to King's murder?

Mrs. Elliot split her class into two groups by the color of their eyes. She told her students that those who had brown eyes were smarter, better behaved, and in every way superior to the blue-eyed kids in the class. Because they were unarguably better, brown-eyed kids were given the best seats in the class. They got extra recess time and second helpings of hot lunch. They were allowed to use the drinking fountain in the classroom.

Blue-eyed students were forced to wear collars identifying which group they were in more easily, and they were repeatedly told how the brown-eyed students were superior to them. In addition to having less time at recess, blue-eyed kids weren't allowed to use any of the playground equipment. They were always placed last in line, and instead of the drinking fountain, they were forced to drink tap water from disposable cups (but they weren't allowed to throw them away because everyone knows that blue-eyed children are wasteful).

Mrs. Elliot wanted to help kids experience what it felt like to be discriminated against, but she was actually horrified by what happened. Students in each group started acting like the brown-eyed/blue-eyed lie was true. Brown-eyed kids looked down on blue-eyed kids and called them names. Blue-eyed kids took longer to do their schoolwork than they had the day before.

On the following day, Mrs. Elliot admitted she lied when she said brown-eyed children are smarter, better behaved, and superior. Everyone knows, she said, that blue-eyed kids are smarter, better behaved, and superior in every way. The results were the same in reverse.

"I watched what had been marvelous, cooperative, wonderful, thoughtful children turn into nasty, vicious, discriminating little third-graders in a space of fifteen minutes," said Mrs. Elliott. She says she realized then that she had created a classroom-sized model of the whole society.

At the end of the two-day exercise, Mrs. Elliot talked

through the experience with her students. She asked how it felt to be told they were better than other kids, how it felt to be treated differently. She then asked how the kids would treat someone with a different skin color.

In an interview for the PBS program *FRONTLINE*, Mrs. Elliot said, "After you do this exercise, when the debriefing starts, when the pain is over and they're all back together, you find out how society could be if we really believed all this stuff that we preach, if we really acted that way, you could feel as good about one another as those kids feel about one another after this exercise is over. You create instant cousins," said Elliott. "The kids said over and over, 'We're kind of like a family now.' They found out how to hurt one another and they found out how it feels to be hurt in that way and they refuse to hurt one another in that way again."[3]

The scientific study of race has changed a lot since Dr. Samuel Morton's mistaken theories about skull sizes, but people still treat minor differences as major reasons to hate. There is more to learn. Let's keep going.

Questions to Consider

- What does it mean to say that race exists only because people *think* it does?
- In what ways do you take your own race for granted?
- How would it feel to be treated differently because of the color of your eyes?

---

3. www.pbs.org/wgbh/frontline/article/introduction-2/.

CHAPTER 4

The Bible on Race and Ethnicity

Understanding the science of skin color is great, and realizing that it is no more significant than eye color is important, but what does God have to say about race and racism?

The Bible was written over the course of hundreds of years by dozens of different authors in various cultures and contexts. It doesn't speak of race the same way we talk about it today. When Bible translations use the word *race*, they generally mean it in one of two ways.

The first way the Bible talks about race refers to the "human race." It is usually meant to highlight everyone's common humanity. For instance, some Bibles translate the Hebrew word *adam* as "human race." "And he said to the human race, 'The fear of the Lord—that is wisdom, and to shun evil is understanding'" (Job 28:28). In this example, *race* refers to all human beings without exception. Wisdom, defined in this passage as "the fear of the Lord," is something for the entire human race—no matter what their ethnicity or skin color might be.

English translations of the Bible also use the term *race* to point out the difference between those who believe in Jesus Christ as their savior and those who do not. First Peter 2:9 (ESV) says, "But you are a chosen race, a royal priesthood, a holy nation, a people for his own possession, that you may proclaim the excellencies of him who called you out of darkness into his marvelous light." In this instance, the term *race*, from the Greek word *genos*, does not refer to a person's skin color or other physical features. The word simply means people who are part of God's new holy nation, the church, through faith in Jesus Christ.

Even though the Bible doesn't talk about race in the same way we use it today, it still has plenty to say about how people should relate to one another across cultural and ethnic differences.

It is important to remember that the individuals and groups discussed in the Bible came from diverse ethnic backgrounds. There are Egyptians, Israelites, Hittites, Cushites, and Jebusites, just to name a few. In the New Testament, when the Holy Spirit came upon the apostles at Pentecost, those who were gathered spoke in languages representing more than a dozen different nations and people groups (Acts 2:9–11). So even though the Bible does not use modern racial categories like "Black" and "white," it has a lot to teach us about how to relate to people who are different from us.

In fact, having so many different people groups was God's plan from the beginning. In Genesis 1, it says that God created mankind—the human race—in God's own image. This belief is the foundation for the basic equality of all peoples.

After Adam and Eve ate the forbidden fruit, God pronounced a curse on the serpent who tempted mankind to sin but promised to rescue the people of God—this is the "good news" or the "gospel." He said in Genesis 3:15, "I will put enmity between you and the woman, and between your off-spring and hers; he will crush your head, and you will strike his heel." There is nothing in this passage to suggest that salvation will in any way be limited or applied differently to people with different skin colors, languages, or positions in society. Indeed, the passage leads us to believe that since Eve would become the "mother of all the living," the promise of salvation will be open to any of her children, to people of all future ethnic groups (Gen. 3:20).

Further along, in Genesis 12, God makes the ethnically diverse character of the good news even clearer. When God speaks to Abram, God makes a promise: "I will make you into a great nation, and I will bless you; I will make your name great, and you will be a blessing. I will bless those who bless you, and whoever curses you I will curse; and all peoples on earth will be blessed through you" (Gen. 12:2–3). In these verses, God promises that through Abram's offspring—children, grand-children, great-grandchildren, and so on—God will bless all the families of the earth.

But that's in the Old Testament. What about in the New Testament, when Jesus comes on the scene?

In the gospel of Luke, we meet a man named Simeon. When Mary and Joseph bring the baby Jesus to the temple, Simeon sees Jesus and says, "My eyes have seen your salvation, which you have prepared in the sight of all nations: a light for revelation to the Gentiles, and the glory of your people Israel" (Luke 2:30–32). Simeon recognizes Jesus as the long-awaited savior who would break down boundaries between nations and people groups.

Jesus himself, in his parting words to his disciples before he rises into heaven, says to them, "You will receive power when the Holy Spirit comes on you; and you will be my witnesses in Jerusalem, and in all Judea and Samaria, and to the ends of the earth" (Acts 1:8). Jesus commands his followers to share the good news in ever-expanding circles, growing from the Jewish capital to faraway nations and people of every ethnicity. Although the good news hasn't finished spreading throughout the world, God does give us a preview.

I love watching previews for upcoming movies, and the best ones give you an idea of what the movie is about, getting you excited for when it finally comes out. God's preview of the perfect, united future comes in the book of Revelation, when Jesus shows his disciple John a peek at the heavenly church: "After this I looked, and there before me was a great multitude that no one could count, from every nation, tribe, people and language, standing before the throne and before the Lamb. They were wearing white robes and were holding palm branches in their hands" (Rev. 7:9).

From beginning to end, from Genesis to Revelation, it was always God's plan to form a multiracial, multiethnic community of worshipers who will spend eternity living in harmony with God and each other. Diversity is God's "Plan A" for the church.

In order to fight racism, people who fight for racial justice must understand how deep and wide God's deliverance is and how the Lord's all-encompassing love is for all peoples.

The Image of God and Race

Sheets of rain drenched Memphis on February 1, 1968. But rain or shine, the garbage trucks had to roll. Two Black sanitation workers, Echol Cole and Robert Walker, took shelter in the back of an old garbage truck to wait out the worst of the downpour. But the truck was long overdue for repair. A wiring malfunction caused the hydraulic compressor in the back of the truck to engage. Cole and Walker could not get free of the truck in time. The two men were crushed to death in the back of the garbage truck.

After the disaster, Black sanitation workers went on strike, refusing to work until the city's leaders gave them the better working conditions, safer equipment, and higher pay they had been asking to have for years. Now with the deaths of two of their friends, a major movement around these rights issues began, one that eventually brought Martin Luther King Jr. to Memphis for what would be his last campaign. Throughout the strike, the sanitation workers used a simple phrase to communicate their core motivation: "I am a man."

At different times throughout the struggle for Black freedom in the United States, activists have argued that equal rights should be given to all people because of our shared humanity. Phrases such as "I am a man" express Black people's insistence that they be treated as fully human—the same as white people. As the **Black Power movement** became more widespread in the late 1960s, the phrases

> **Black Power movement**: A historical period in the 1960s and 1970s when people promoted the idea that Black people should be able to lead their own communities by electing officials, owning businesses, fostering a positive sense of self, and resisting racism

"Black is beautiful" and "It is so beautiful to be black" showed up on signs at protests and rallies. In 1971, a Black activist named Jesse Jackson appeared on *Sesame Street* and recited a poem called "I Am Somebody." It soon became a catchphrase for civil rights activism.

And in more recent years, the hashtag #BlackLivesMatter has been popularized by activists who believe that people of African descent have just as much value as anyone else.

All of these phrases—"I am a man," "Black is beautiful," "#BlackLivesMatter"—are grounded in the fact that we are all made in the image of God. Every claim for equal rights and freedom comes from the reality that God made every one of us with dignity and value.

In the first chapter of the first book of the Bible, God communicates the unity and equality that goes into all people. Genesis 1:26–27 provides the basis for this doctrine:

> Then God said, "Let us make mankind in our image, in our likeness, so that they may rule over the fish in the sea and the birds in the sky, over the livestock and all the wild animals, and over all the creatures that move along the ground." So God created mankind in his own image, in the image of God he created them; male and female he created them.

Of course, we're not *exactly* like God. We are not all-powerful (omnipotent) and we don't know all things (omniscient). But God has crowned human beings with glory and honor (Ps. 8:5). As God's image-bearers, all people have God-given worth and importance.

God's fingerprints rest upon every single person. No one was left out. The image of God extends to Black and white people, men and women, rich and poor, people behind bars and free, queer and straight, documented and undocumented, nondisabled and disabled, powerful and oppressed. All people equally bear the likeness of God and should be valued greater than anything else God has created and in a way that can never be lessened.

If human beings are the image of God, then that image includes our skin color. Correctly understanding what the Bible means about the image of God means knowing that Black people and other people of color do not have to "become white" in any sense in order to be treated with respect.

Too often in our society, racial and ethnic minorities are forced to change important pieces of their identity in order to have the same opportunities as others. Whether it is one's pattern of speech, clothing, hairstyle, zip code, schooling, or interests, the message to people of color is, "In order for us to accept you,

> **God does not mistake unity for uniformity. God celebrates diversity.**

your color and your culture must go. You must become white." But the image of God teaches that no part of the way God created us has to be abandoned in order to gain the respect of other image-bearers. God does not mistake unity—being together no matter how different we are—for uniformity—being the same as everyone else. God celebrates diversity.

Bearing God's Image Takes a Community

What's your name? That's such an important question because it helps people know who you are and why you are different from the next person. And isn't it annoying when someone pronounces your name incorrectly? At the same time, you're not just an individual person. You are part of a group as well. Maybe you're on a sports team, or in a club, or part of a homeroom class. Groups are important too.

Human beings do not simply bear God's image as individuals but as groups. Each group—people who speak Spanish, who live in New Zealand, who are of African descent, and more—with their various languages, dress, foods, clothing, and customs reveals a small part of God's infinite diversity. The kingdom of God is described as a banquet to which all, especially those who usually get left out and overlooked, are invited (Luke 14). Perhaps this banquet will be a potluck. Ethiopians will bring injera, Nigerians jollof, Jamaicans goat curry, and Koreans kimchee. Like a communal banquet that highlights the best parts of different cultures, the heavenly congregation will display the magnificent diversity of God's people.

No single group can reflect the glory of God by itself. We need the diversity of all nations and tribes to paint a more complete portrait of God's splendor. Differences are invitations to curiosity and not reasons to bully people. But the sad reality is that racism tries to destroy the image of God among certain people groups. Historically, people of African descent have been made out to be less than human by those who believe themselves to be superior.

In 1900, the American Book and Bible House published a book by Charles Carroll entitled *"The Negro a Beast"; or, "In the Image of God?"* Carroll and those who agreed with him said that white people descended from Adam and Eve but "negroes" originally descended from animals. "If the White was created 'in the image of God,' then the Negro was made after some other model. And a glance at the Negro indicates the model; his very appearance suggests the ape." Carroll compared Black people to apes (and it's never okay to call someone names that compare them to animals) and he believed that Black people had been designed by God to serve the white man.

During this same period of US history, images that were designed to make fun of Black people entered popular culture, like plays, movies, and magazine ads. The pickaninny, an insulting name in itself, was an offensive picture of a Black child. Artists drew the pickaninny in ragged clothes, with messy hair and big lips and noses, and made them look stupid. Similarly, the "mammy" character was a fictionalized Black woman dressed in the apron of a household servant, who always seemed to be smiling and laughing—like the Aunt Jemima character who used to be on the front of pancake syrup bottles. These images never showed how hard Black women worked to serve their white employers or what other hardships they suffered.

Today, seeing these images has become rarer, but racism remains baked into the way society is set up. The white hoods and burning crosses of the KKK are a no-no, but instead we see poor Black and brown people shuffled into inner-city communities. Racism today comes in the form of **mass incarceration** and police brutality toward people of color. You can find it in

Mass incarceration: Locking up a large population of people

the ongoing and widening racial wealth gap, where white people are typically better off financially than Black people. In 2020, it took a massive uprising for racial justice to finally get brands like Quaker Oats' Aunt Jemima to acknowledge and change their logos away from their racial stereotype origins.

Native American activists and their allies have campaigned for years for sports teams to remove racist images and symbols used as mascots. The stereotypes associated with being the "model minority"[1] continue to be thrust on people of Asian

---

1. For a deeper look at the topic of the model minority, turn to Additional Articles at the back of this book.

descent. In every area of society—from politics, to economics, to pop culture—the lessening of the image of God in people of color continues. The fight is not over.

God's image cannot be found in any single community. We can't pretend God prefers one race over another or ignore the cries for equity from those who have been told they don't matter. Our actions must match our understanding that God is best represented by a diverse community.

Questions to Consider

- What does the variety of skin colors in the world tell us about our Creator?
- How is the kingdom of God like a potluck?
- What are some ways white people have sought to make less of Black people through images and advertising?

CHAPTER 5

Racial Justice in Action: Confronting Racism Where It Lives

Understanding the science of race—we're more alike than different—and what the Bible says about God's image—our differences show the diverse nature of God—should motivate us to keep learning. Let's look at a few strategies to learn how race affects the people around us and call our racism for what it is.

Have a Conversation About Race and Ethnicity

You are old enough to recognize how people from different races and ethnic backgrounds are treated differently by society. You've probably also seen that talking about these differences can sometimes make people uncomfortable. Maybe you've had questions about people from different races, but you've been told to quiet down, that asking those questions is rude. Actually, being able to have conversations about racial differences is important to understanding how to see the image of God in everyone.

Race can be a touchy subject. There are a lot of ways to talk about it, and many of those ways may hurt people's feelings. You might think of all the mistakes you could make and decide just to keep quiet. But I encourage you to ask questions!

If you want to know a little more about someone's experience, food, clothing, or views, don't always hold it in. Ask someone, especially a teacher, parent, or other trusted adult. Say something like, "I don't mean to sound rude, but I am really curious about _____. Can you tell me more about it?" Or you could say, "I saw something on the news or with one of my friends today that had to do with race, but I'm not sure I understand. Could I tell you about it and get your thoughts?"

Asking questions of others and yourself in a group setting is really important. The group can be people from your own race or ethnicity or a mix of different people. Ask:

- How have you been impacted by your race or ethnicity?
- When or how have you thought about your own race?
- When was the first time you interacted with someone from a different racial identity?
- What does discrimination feel like?

It can be hard to be honest about painful memories, but if you each promise to respect each other, and not laugh or make fun of each other, these kinds of questions lead to greater trust and understanding.

It's possible that white people may be mistrusted by people

of color due to the history of whites dehumanizing or excluding them. Keep that in mind, and keep trying. The best way to earn trust is by being consistently trustworthy.

When you are able to gather a diverse group of people, don't dominate the discussion. This is a time to listen and learn. Work on developing relationships by talking about common interests. The more comfortable people are in your group, the more freely they will be able to discuss their feelings and thoughts about issues of race and ethnicity.

Listen for how people answer the same questions differently depending on their individual experiences and their racial or ethnic background. There is also a chance you or someone else may make a mistake and say something harmful or offensive. Relax. This is part of the process. If you find yourself saying something offensive in this group, talk about what you said and why it was wrong. Then apologize . . . and be prepared to forgive others as well. Use the mistake as a learning opportunity and keep trying.

And remember, if you're Black or a person of color, you do not always have to answer

> Unity happens when diversity is embraced as God's original plan for the world and the church.

everyone's questions. If the topic is too painful or you are just too tired, it's fine to say, "Thanks for your question, but I need some time."

If the group is a Christian group, feel free to discuss the things you've learned from this book about how God treats race. Explain what you've studied and listen to other people's stories. Unity happens when diversity is embraced as God's original plan for the world and the church.

Learn from "the Least of These"

In 1949, a Black man named Howard Thurman (we'll learn more about him later in this book) made a case for Christians to see how Jesus identified with those the Bible calls "the least of these" (Matt. 25:40, 45). Instead of hanging out with the rich and powerful people of his day, Jesus sought out the poor and powerless.

Think about that for a moment. Jesus, who was God in the flesh, the owner of everything, the most powerful being in the universe, wanted to hang out with people who had been rejected. Jesus, the coolest guy ever to walk the planet, came into the cafeteria of earth and did not sit at the "cool kids" table. Instead Jesus sat at the table with all the "rejects"— the unpopular, the uncool, the ones who get picked on and laughed at, the people who look different, the ones who don't have a lot of money. In other words, Jesus became friends with people like you and me.

Any growth in how people think about race from a Christian perspective must include learning from people who know what it means to be overlooked and kept down. It should be obvious, but people often need to be reminded that listening to others doesn't necessarily mean you agree with everything they say. On the other hand, refusing to listen to someone shuts down the opportunity to learn new things or see old things in new ways.

Treat Racism as It Should Be Treated: Like a Sin

The city of Pacifica, California, lies on the West Coast between San Francisco and Half Moon Bay and is home to the Pacific

Bay Christian School, whose elementary school and middle and high schools are spread out over thirty-seven acres (that's a lot of land!). The school's mission is "to be a community of Christian scholarship and discipleship that nurtures our students' growth in faith, knowledge, and virtue." The school has come a long way since it was founded as Alma Heights Christian Academy in 1955.

The school was originally named for Alma White, the founder of the Pillar of Fire Church. Alma was a forceful advocate for women's equality, but she's an example that people can do both good and bad things. Unfortunately, Alma was just as outspoken in her attacks on racial minorities. She spoke at gatherings of the Ku Klux Klan and wrote in a newspaper called *The Good Citizen*, "Where people seek for social equality between the black and white races they violate the edicts of Holy Writ and every social and moral code." She said Black and white people being together was a sin!

Alma Heights Christian Academy was founded as a "segregation academy." In the years following the Supreme Court's ruling in *Brown v. Board of Education of Topeka* (which we'll learn more about later in this book), white parents who were concerned about Black and white kids mixing in public schools started private schools meant to keep Black students out.

While many schools that were founded as segregation academies now have official statements saying they'll admit students of any race, color, national or ethnic origin, even today many have not made efforts to overcome their racist history.

Pacific Bay Christian School, or PacBay, stands out as an example of an institution that *has* wrestled with its racist past and committed to do more than make statements. In 1997, the school hired Dr. Michael Chen, its first principal of color. As a condition of Chen's hiring, the school had to agree to change its name from Alma Heights.

A name change was just the beginning. The advisory council of the newly named PacBay took a deep look at what the school taught, how it hired teachers and staff, and what decisions had kept white people focused in the center of their priorities. As Chen said in an article by the *Hechinger Report*, the effects of white supremacy are everywhere; it's "in the air we breathe."[1]

Things only change when people are willing to recognize the sin of racism. The root of the problem is the failure to recognize racism as sin.

In a post on the PacBay website from June 4, 2020, Dr. Chen wrote, "For the sake of the flourishing of all of our students, we must call out the sin of racism prophetically, minister humbly as a community to all those who are hurting, and act meaningfully as a collective witness of God's justice (Amos 5)."

Some people love chocolate. Some people can't stand it. No worries. It's just a preference. You can hate chocolate and I can crave it, and we can still get along. Racism is not like that. Racism is not simply a difference of opinion. Racism is sin. But too often we treat racism like a preference, as if it's okay for some people to be racist and some people not to be racist, just like some people like chocolate and some don't. This is unacceptable. Racism means individuals are failing

---

1. Bekah McNeel, "Some Christian Schools Are Finally Grappling with Their Racist Past and Segregated Present," *The Hechinger Report*, August 26, 2020, https://hechingerreport .org/christian-schools-grapple-with-demographic-change-and-their-racist-past/.

to recognize God's image in their fellow human beings, and the body of Christ—the whole Church—suffers when sin is allowed to go on.

Questions to Consider

- Who are some people you can commit to having a conversation about race with? How can you form a group to have these conversations?
- Why do you think people don't treat racism as a sin?

Frederick's Fight

When I was growing up, I *loved* to read. I still do. But when I was around ten years old, I started reading Dungeons and Dragons books. My favorite series was called Dragonlance, and it had more than thirty books in the series, all at least three hundred pages long. I read nonstop. I loved diving into the fantasy world of elves, wizards, dragons, and epic wars. It is because I was a reader at a very young age that I became a writer as an adult. But reading was more than that. I was very shy during elementary and middle school and I didn't have many friends. Oftentimes, books would be my only company and comfort in my loneliness. Honestly, I don't know what I would have done as a kid if it wasn't for books.

Maybe you're a bibliophile too. Don't worry, I'm not calling you a name—bibliophile literally means "book lover" or someone who loves books. If you love books, just imagine if you weren't even allowed to learn how to read. That was the reality for most enslaved Black people.

Frederick Augustus Washington Bailey was born in Maryland around 1818. He never knew when his actual birthday was. Frederick's mother, Harriet Bailey, was an enslaved Black woman. That meant Frederick was enslaved as well.

While he was still a baby, Frederick was taken from his mother, who was sold to a farm about twelve miles away. It was common in those times to remove a Black baby from their mother to be raised by an enslaved woman who was too old to work in the fields. This arrangement kept women working even into their old age—no such thing as a quiet retirement for enslaved Black people—and the slave holders thought that neither the baby nor the mother could develop a bond, so they wouldn't be too upset when one of them is sold far away.

Of course, this didn't stop Harriet from visiting Frederick occasionally.

Later in life, Frederick wrote, "She made her journeys to see me in the night, travelling the whole distance on foot, after the performance of her day's work. She was a field hand, and a whipping is the penalty of not being in the field at sunrise . . . I do not recollect of ever seeing my mother by the light of day. She was with me in the night. She would lie down with me, and get me to sleep, but long before I waked she was gone."[1]

Though Frederick's mother obviously loved him, he didn't get the opportunity to grow up with her. Harriet Bailey died when Frederick was six or seven years old.

Around this time, Frederick was sent to live with his mother's old master, Aaron Anthony, at a **plantation** called Wye House Farm. The plantation once

> **Plantation**: A large area of farmland that was owned by a wealthy person who relied on the labor of poorer people, typically enslaved Black people, to plant and harvest crops

spanned 20,000 acres (imagine 15,151.5 football fields) and enslaved between seven hundred to over a thousand people at a time.

Frederick worked on the plantation for about two years before

---

1. From *Narrative of the Life of Frederick Douglass.*

he was given to Lucretia Auld, who passed him along to her brother-in-law, Hugh, in Baltimore. It was in Baltimore that Frederick's life would profoundly change, equipping him with the tools he needed to change the world. Because Hugh Auld's wife, Sophia, broke an age-old rule for slave holders: she taught young Frederick the alphabet.

Why was there a rule against teaching slaves the alphabet? Because an educated enslaved person is dangerous. They might learn to see the injustice of their own condition and work to change it.

Using the little knowledge he was given, Frederick Augustus Washington Bailey taught himself how to read and write. Soon, he was teaching other enslaved people to read, using the Bible as a textbook. When his owners discovered his efforts to educate others, he was sent to another owner, Edward Covey.

Covey was known for mistreating slaves. Now sixteen years old, Frederick felt Covey's cruelty firsthand, receiving regular whippings from his new slave holder. The treatment almost broke his spirit, but Frederick had many more things to accomplish before he was finished.

At the age of twenty, and after a number of attempts, Frederick finally escaped slavery with the help of his future wife, Anna Murray. The two were married in New York but moved to New Bedford, Massachusetts, shortly afterward. To help them avoid capture, Frederick and Anna took a new last name for themselves.

Frederick Bailey became Frederick Douglass.

In the years that followed, Douglass used the reading and writing skills he acquired early on and wrote about his life as an enslaved Black man. He spoke against slavery. He spoke about all people having the right to vote. His story was an inspiration for many to do something about the institution of slavery.

Frederick Douglass crossed the ocean and spoke in Ireland and Great Britain about the evils of slavery and the hypocrisy of the United States' claim to be the "land of the free."

In one speech, he said, "What is to be thought of a nation boasting of its liberty, boasting of its humanity, boasting of its Christianity, boasting of its love of justice and purity, and yet having within its own borders three millions of persons denied by law the right of marriage?"[2]

During the Civil War, Frederick spoke up for the right of soon-to-be-freed Black Americans to vote. After the war, he held many government positions, always working for the betterment of other Black people.

None of this might have happened if Frederick hadn't been taught the alphabet by a former slave holder's wife. Education proved to be a dangerous thing to people who benefitted from keeping others in a place of servitude instead of a place of equity.

Frederick Douglass died in 1895, but he lived long enough to see the passage of the Fifteenth Amendment, which stated that voting rights could not be "denied or abridged by the United States or by any state on account of race, color, or previous condition of servitude." Black men (though not women . . . yet) finally had the legal right to vote.

Of course, having the legal standing to vote and *being allowed* to vote are two different things, and time would prove that the struggle of Black people for equity was far from over.

As we dive into the history of race relations in America, my hope is that you will use your education as Frederick Douglass used his, breaking down the barriers that keep people apart and fighting for fair treatment for all people.

---

2. From Frederick Douglass, "My Bondage and My Freedom," a speech given at Finsbury Chapel, Moorfields, England, on May 12, 1846.

CHAPTER 6

How to Study the History of Race

History is filled with amazing stories of people like Frederick Douglass who overcome obstacles in order to make life better for everyone.

James Baldwin—a Black writer from the mid-twentieth century, whose work has influenced many thought leaders and other writers—reflected on the importance of history in his pointed and insightful essay, "Unnameable Objects, Unspeakable Crimes." Baldwin explained, "For history, as nearly no one seems to know, is not merely something to be read. And it does not refer merely, or even principally, to the past. On the contrary, the great force of history comes from the fact that we carry it within us, are unconsciously controlled by it in many ways, and history is literally present in all that we do." History is alive.

In order to effectively fight racism, we must learn from the past. You may have heard the saying, "If you don't learn from the past, you are doomed to repeat it." But historians are quick to point out that history does not, in fact, repeat itself.

Historical events are too caught up in the conditions of the moment, too influenced by so many different factors, they can never simply repeat. But history does rhyme. We can hear the rhythms of the past in the present. Learning about history is more than learning about what has happened before—it is about understanding what is happening now.

Over the next few chapters, we're going to look at the history of racism from the time of Christopher Columbus to the present. By understanding how we got to where we are, my hope is that you'll have a better understanding of how issues of race are currently playing out in your community, nation, and the world.

Why Study History?

History is context—the setting and conditions that help explain an event or a person's words and actions. In seminary, my professors taught me that in order to read the Bible well you have to know the context of the part of the Bible you are reading. I learned to ask whether the passage is poetry or story-driven, who the authors were, when they were writing, and to whom. What other events were happening at the time, and what did the words mean in the original Hebrew, Aramaic, or Greek language? All of this is important to help readers understand what the Bible actually says. The same is true when it comes to learning history. To learn history is to learn context.

When a white police officer killed Mike Brown, a Black teenager, and made #BlackLivesMatter a national rallying cry, I, like many others, tried to figure out why the event happened. How was it that a mostly white police force was responsible for patrolling a mostly Black neighborhood? Why was the community of Ferguson so segregated in the first place? How was this tragedy connected to so many others like it?

As I tried to understand our present-day context, I found that historians often had the most helpful information. They explained how cities forced Black people to live in certain neighborhoods separated from white people. They talked about the origins of the police force and their connections to **slave patrols**. I learned from historians that the past is a key to understanding and fighting racism today.

Slave patrols: Groups of armed white men who policed enslaved Black people and who captured Black people who escaped slavery

We need to study history not simply to know more about the past but to know more about ourselves. History is about identity. Rightly remembering the stories we are all a part of is a way of seeing how we fit into the bigger story. History tells us who and where we come from, how the people and events before us have shaped us, and what kind of actions we need to take in order to pursue a more racially just future. Without a sense of history we lose our sense of self.

CHAPTER 7

The History of Race in America: Where It All Started

"Discovering" the New World

After about two months of sailing, Christopher Columbus and his bedraggled crew stumbled onto the shores of the Americas (North, Central, and South America) in 1492. Of course, Columbus and his men did not walk onto uninhabited land. When they arrived, they found a place vibrant with plants and animals as well as sophisticated communities of **indigenous people** who had dwelled there since before written memory. Columbus's arrival marked the beginning of an era of European colonization—one motivated by money and based on unpaid labor.

> **Indigenous people**: The earliest known people to live in a specific region

From the very start, many European colonists looked down on darker-skinned people. During his first voyage, Columbus wrote in his journal, "[The indigenous inhabitants] should be good servants and intelligent, for I observed that they quickly took in what was said to them, and I believe that they would easily be made Christians, as it appeared to me that they had no religion."

To Columbus and his followers, the people they encountered would make "good servants." Indigenous people were not considered as smart or socially developed as the Europeans. According to some, their only value was their ability to do what the Europeans wanted.

Also, in the mind of Columbus and others, indigenous people didn't have the sophistication to develop their own religious beliefs. Europeans failed to acknowledge the long-standing, well-developed religious beliefs and practices of the people they met. Instead, they saw these people as blank slates on which Christian missionaries could write the gospel.

This tendency for Christians to think of someone else's beliefs as simplistic or backwards doesn't come across as a loving invitation to know Jesus as their savior, but rather as thinking someone is less valuable or not as intelligent because they believe differently. It means that they are seen as somehow having less of the image of God in them than Europeans do. Unfortunately, this view can be found throughout the American church's history.

For the next 150 years, European colonists established settlements in North America. Native Americans resisted colonization, but they got sick with European diseases, were frequently betrayed, and were killed in battle. As the demands for raw materials such as corn, tobacco, and animal products grew, so did the European colonies. To meet these growing calls for goods from European countries, colonizers in North America increasingly turned to slavery.

The Transatlantic Slave Trade

Over the next three hundred years, the transatlantic slave trade transported more than ten million Africans to the Americas in a **displacement** of epic scale. About two million people died on the voyages. The human cost in terms of suffering, disrespect, and death caused by this cruel trade can never be fully grasped, but the experience is often misunderstood or downplayed today.

> **Displacement**: The forced relocation of people from their homeland to another place

Ships would sail from England, France, Spain, Portugal, and other nations to the western coast of Africa. There, the Europeans would either trade with local African tribes for slaves captured in war or kidnap their own slaves.

Enslavers marched their captives sometimes hundreds of miles to the western coast of Africa. The slaves were tied together or had their necks clamped with wooden yokes. Many died before they could reach their destination. Those who survived were taken to fortress-like structures called "factories" until it was time for them to be loaded onto ships. Slave traders separated families and tribes so the Africans could not band together and rebel. Finally, sometimes after months of waiting, the slaves shuffled onto ships called "slavers" bound for the Americas.

Conditions were even worse on the ship. You might be thinking, "Well, I would just jump off the ship and swim back to land." Slave traders thought of that. So they often shackled Africans together to prevent them from jumping overboard or rebelling. African slaves endured a horrific journey, which became known as the "middle passage," from their native land to South America, the Caribbean Islands, or North America.

It normally took two or three months to cross the Atlantic, but for some the journey lasted up to six months.

Even after surviving the middle passage, Africans were only beginning to experience the horrors of slavery. Ships usually landed at a port in the Caribbean. Then, slave ship captains did their best to sell their cargo as quickly as possible.

Upon purchase, the newly arrived Africans were "seasoned" to prepare them for their lives of bondage and labor in the Americas. Seasoning involved adapting to a different climate and new foods. It also involved teaching the Africans a new language, usually French, Spanish, or English. Africans were trained for their work, which was typically agricultural and involved plowing, hoeing, and weeding from sunup to sundown. This process took its toll. As many as one-third of African slaves died within their first three years in the Americas.

The Colonial Era

The United States of America began as a group of European colonies. Colonization of the "New World"—new to the Europeans, not to the millions of indigenous peoples who already inhabited the Americas—began in the fifteenth century and continued for hundreds of years. The colonial era for the United States roughly began with the English colony at Jamestown, Virginia, in 1606, and lasted until about 1776 with the Declaration of Independence.

In 1619, a Dutch trading ship named the *White Lion* landed off the coast of Virginia with "20 and odd" Africans. The arrival of these enslaved women and men wasn't expected, but it was readily accepted by the British colonists who lived there.

The *White Lion* had stolen the Africans from a Portuguese slave trading ship called *São João Bautista*, or *Saint John the Baptist*, and they were looking for a place to sell their human cargo.

But these were not the first enslaved Africans Europeans brought to the Americas. Prior to the arrival of Africans in the British Virginia colony, Europeans had been transporting enslaved Africans to other places in the region for more than a hundred years. Haiti and Jamaica, as well as South American countries such as Brazil, used millions of Africans to work on farms producing rice, sugar, and coffee.

In North America, slavery developed differently but no less cruelly. In some cases, Europeans treated Africans as indentured servants—workers bound to an employer for a certain time, usually to pay off a debt. Indentured servants could marry, save money, and eventually work themselves out of servitude.

The women and men who arrived on the Virginia coast in 1619 had names like Angelo and Pedro and were likely Catholic. After a number of years, they may have gained their liberty. As early as 1623, two Africans named Anthony and Isabella married. They had a son, William, who was baptized as an Anglican and likely born free.

By the mid-seventeenth century, some Africans lived as free people and worked in a variety of different jobs. A few became wealthy enough to own land and buy enslaved Africans themselves. The life of an indentured servant was not a desirable one, but it was not always permanent, nor was it limited to Africans. Indigenous people and Europeans could become indentured servants too.

The practice of indentured servitude gradually gave way

to slavery, and Europeans preferred Africans as laborers over other Europeans or the indigenous Americans. Much of the transition toward slavery happened because people wanted to save money. In slavery, people were not people, they were property. You could buy or sell a human being just like buying or selling a car. Purchasing a person was expensive. But it was worth the price to slaveholders if they could buy a person and then keep them laboring for decades at very little additional cost.

Since slave holders could make lots of money forcing people to labor and then not paying them, slavery became more common than indentured servitude. The transition to slavery as the preference was made official with Virginia's slave codes. In 1705, Virginia's law-making body made a declaration that would impact Black women and men in America for generations.

"All servants imported and brought into the Country . . . who were not Christians in their native Country . . . shall be accounted and be slaves. All Negro, mulatto and Indian slaves within this dominion . . . shall be held to be real estate. If any slave resist his master . . . correcting such slave, and shall happen to be killed in such correction . . . the master shall be free of all punishment . . . as if such accident never happened."

The slave codes determined that a child was born slave or free based solely on the mother's status. They mandated slavery for life with no hope of **emancipation**. The codes denied

Emancipation: Being set free

enslaved people's legal rights, required slaves to get permission to leave their master's property, forbade marriage between enslaved people, and made it illegal for them to carry weapons. The slave codes also defined enslaved Africans not as human beings but as chattel—private property on the same level as cows, sheep, and other livestock.

Once the slave code was passed in 1705, if a slave had any kind of disagreement with her or his master, the slave holder could deliver any punishment they wanted to—including death—without fear of any legal harm to themselves. The Virginia slave codes were used to create similar codes throughout the rest of the New World's British colonies.

When Christopher Columbus launched the European efforts to claim American land, he and others helped spread the idea that people with darker skin were designed to serve those with lighter skin. That idea, along with people's greed for money, led to the transatlantic slave trade, which was soon legally protected in order to help the rich get richer and justify the notion that enslaving Black people was actually a good thing.

But change was in the air. The American colonies were growing and they started to resent being ruled by kings and queens across the Atlantic. While freedom for slaves was still the furthest thing from their minds, these colonists wanted freedom for themselves.

CHAPTER 8

The History of Race in America: An Uneasy Compromise

The Revolutionary War

In the years leading up to 1776 and the US Declaration of Independence, British colonists in America grew increasingly frustrated with being subject to what they called "taxation without representation."

Basically, the colonists didn't like the fact that people across the Atlantic were making decisions about how much money to charge them in taxes, since no one was asking the colonists what they thought would be fair. The irony of this patriot rallying cry is that the enslaved Black people who made life in the colonies sustainable—and whose labor made the colonies worth ruling from afar—experienced far worse than the taxation on things like tea, paint, and paper, yet they also had no representation or voice in the circumstances of their lives.

Setting this point aside for a moment, let's discuss some key Black figures and events in the years surrounding the Revolutionary War.

Indigenous American and African blood flowed through the veins of Crispus Attucks. During the Boston Massacre of 1770, his blood spilled onto the streets along with four other men in one of the events that led up to the Revolutionary War.

We don't know a lot about Attucks' life, but he was likely born in the early 1720s near Natick, Massachusetts. He endured life in slavery, but in 1750 he escaped his master and made a living for himself as a sailor. Twenty years later he joined a crowd of Boston residents who exchanged heated words with a small group of British soldiers. The conflict turned violent, and a soldier shot and killed Attucks.

However mythical his story has become, it makes a lot of sense to talk about Attucks when you talk about American independence. He took freedom into his own hands just like the colonists believed they were doing. He represented the racial diversity of America and stands for indigenous women and men as much as Black Americans. What's more, he died for a nation that failed to recognize his freedom because of his racial background. Attucks symbolizes that bitter combination of freedom and bondage, racism and patriotism, that characterized the Revolutionary era.

As the colonists were fighting back against British rule, they were also dreaming about what a new nation might look like. What would be its values, ideals, and rules? They began to answer those questions in the founding documents of what would soon become the United States of America.

The Declaration of Independence, first written out by a slaveholder named Thomas Jefferson, captured the spirit of revolution in its opening words. "We hold these truths to be self-evident, that all men are created equal, that they are endowed by their Creator with certain unalienable Rights, that among these are Life, Liberty and the pursuit of Happiness."

But racism was part of the United States even before the nation had officially formed. The color line between Black and white people was written into the founding documents. Thomas Jefferson, like so many of his day, did not consider Black people equal to white people. Few political leaders assumed the noble words of the Declaration of Independence applied to the enslaved.

When Africans in America heard white leaders proclaim natural rights and equality for all, however, they logically applied those statements to their own situation. In a 1773 letter to the Massachusetts General Court, a committee of enslaved individuals wrote, "We cannot but expect your house will again take our deplorable case into serious consideration, and give us that ample relief who, as men, we have a natural right to." In other words, "We ask you again to recognize that we are men like you, created equal to you, and we deserve freedom like you."

The longing for liberty was so strong that Africans in the colonies took up arms—weapons—to pursue it. Some fought for the British on the promise they'd be freed because of their service against the rebellious colonists. They were called Loyalists because they remained loyal to the British side. Other Black people fought for the colonists in America with the hope that if they won the war against the British, then they would also be freed. They were called Patriots.

One of the most famous Black Loyalist fighters was Colonel Tye, an enslaved Black man who escaped a brutal master and used his familiarity with the land to lead daring attacks on Patriot strongholds. Tye took good care of the Black Brigade soldiers under his command and freed enslaved people on the Patriot farms they raided for supplies.

On the other side of the conflict, around five thousand Black men fought with the Patriots, hoping victory would ensure **abolition**. Many served with distinction. The stories of Black Patriots like Peter Salem, James Armistead Lafayette, and the First Rhode Island Regiment demon-strate that Black people were brave and fierce soldiers, especially when they were fighting for their own independence.

> **Abolition**: The end of slavery

No matter which side an enslaved person fought for, the motivation was the same: freedom. But despite the efforts of African-descended people to gain freedom during the American Revolution, the practice of slavery continued long after the war was over.

The Drafting of the Constitution

After the smoke of the Revolutionary War had been blown away by the winds of independence, the political leaders of the colonies set about forming a new nation. Their first task was to write a document outlining how the government would work. In 1781, they ratified, or officially approved, the Articles of Confederation. It quickly became clear that the Articles did not give enough power to any central, or federal, government and they had to be replaced. The result was the Constitutional Convention of 1787, which produced the US Constitution.

To understand what the Constitution is, think about your school's student handbook. Every school has one, and it contains information for parents and family members, as well as all the rules that students have to follow—such as what clothes and jewelry you can wear, what happens if you disrupt class, and who to go to if you have different kinds of problems.

The US Constitution is like a student handbook for citizens in the country. The best student handbooks have the same rules and the same rewards for all students. It would be unfair if the handbook applied to fifth graders but not sixth graders, right? But that's what happened with the US Constitution. It had rules, especially privileges like voting, that only applied to some people—white people—and not to other people like Black people and women. These other groups couldn't always count on the legal protections stated in the Constitution.

The US Constitution doesn't use the words *slave* or *slavery*, yet some scholars argue that it did indeed support slavery. For example, Article IV, Section 2 of the Constitution, states, "No Person held to Service or Labour in one State, under the Laws thereof, escaping into another, shall . . . be discharged from such Service or Labour, but shall be delivered up on Claim of the Party to whom such Service or Labour may be due." This is known as the Fugitive Slave Clause. Although the word *slave* is absent, this section clearly means that any enslaved person who escaped their bondage and crossed state lines from a slave state to a free state had to be returned to his or her owner. Imagine going through all the danger and risk of escaping slavery just to be caught in another state and returned to your slave holder! From the beginning, the Constitution made sure that nowhere in America would be safe for an escaped enslaved person.

Article 1, Section 2, presents another way the founders wrote racism into the US Constitution. This section explains that states with more people got to elect more members to Congress, a governing body in the US capital. Every state wanted to have lots of people so they could have many representatives in government and have more power to get what they wanted for their own state. The problem was figuring out who would "count" in each state. Would enslaved people count the same as white people? Would they not count at all? That number "shall be determined by adding to the whole Number of free Persons, including those bound to Service for a Term of Years and excluding Indians not taxed, three fifths of all other Persons." This clause is more popularly known as the Three-Fifths Compromise.

Why was this clause included, and what did it mean? The Southern government officials and landowners relied on slavery, so they wanted enslaved Black people to count in the official population numbers, which would give those states more representation in Congress. But Northern government officials did not want enslaved people to count—after all, they couldn't vote—and they did not want the South to have more power than states in the North (although, to be clear, slavery benefited people in the North too). They argued for a long time, but neither side could win. So they came up with a deal, a compromise.

Instead of acknowledging the full humanity and citizenship of enslaved Black people, political leaders agreed that each enslaved person would count not as a whole person but as three-fifths of a white citizen. They also agreed to include a sentence that allowed for slavery to continue for at least another twenty years. Slavery was not open for debate again in the United States until 1808.

The Antebellum Era

As you might imagine, the Three-Fifths Compromise and the section of the Constitution that guaranteed the practice of slavery for another twenty years only made racism in the United States a bigger problem in the years to come.

Antebellum is a Latin word meaning "before the war" and refers to the years after the War of 1812 (1812–15) and before the Civil War (1861–65). As states began to rely on each other throughout the Union (the states that made up the US), different locations began to specialize in different things. The North, with its established oceanfront cities focused on industry, focused on making things to sell elsewhere. The South, with land that could easily grow food, focused on farming and agriculture.

By 1815, the main Southern crop grown was cotton. With the inventions of the cotton gin (a simple machine that separates cotton fiber from the seeds) and textile mills (water-powered machines that spun the fibers into usable cloth), slavery was justified as a necessary evil in order to meet the world's demand for cotton goods. In reality, people were getting rich from enslaved people's labor and they didn't want that to end. Plantations grew and enslaved individuals were regularly whipped and beaten to get them to work faster.

It would be a mistake to think that Black people were happy with being enslaved or that they didn't try to fight back. Even though resistance would certainly mean punishment and possibly even death, Black people in America found ways, both small and large, to resist oppression.

Some of them broke tools on purpose to delay their work. Others would set fires or pretend to be sick. Enslaved Blacks pretended to be less intelligent than they were to make enslavers think they were less capable of fighting back or couldn't handle complex work. They sometimes stole food or other items to make up for all the years they worked and didn't get paid. Even learning to read was a form of resistance. Remember the story of Frederick Douglass?

Of course, escape was also a form of resistance. But running away from the plantation meant increased risk, punishment, and perhaps death if recaptured. Plans had to be thought up that were so secret, no white person would catch on. To hide their plans for running away, enslaved Blacks hid messages in their songs. A well-known example is the song "Steal Away," which includes the line "Steal away home to Jesus." Those words had a double meaning and could also be heard as a message to let other enslaved Blacks know when it would be best to escape or "steal away"—meaning run away—from the plantation.

The riskiest form of resistance, which held the highest potential reward, was a slave rebellion. In Saint-Domingue, now known as Haiti, the enslaved Black population of this Caribbean island carried out the first successful slave rebellion of the modern Atlantic world. From 1781 to 1804, enslaved Blacks in France's richest colony rebelled against their enslavers, who were hugely outnumbered, and took the island from their European oppressors. News of the revolution spread around the world and put fear into the hearts of white plantation owners. When enslaved Blacks did attempt rebellion in the United States (Nat Turner's Rebellion is one famous example), forces were quickly assembled to put down the rebellion, and hundreds of enslaved individuals who were suspected of participating—or even wanting to participate—were killed in order to put down any further rebellious ideas.

As Black men and women sought to escape slavery's injustices, tensions were rising in the United States over the issue of slavery itself. Just as the colonies split off from England, states in the South would soon split off from states in the North. The very union of the United States was at the breaking point. And all because of racism.

CHAPTER 9

The History of Race in America: A Country Divided

The Civil War

To this day, the Civil War (1861–65) remains the deadliest war in US history. Historians think that somewhere between 650,000 and 850,000 people died. In the Battle of Gettysburg alone, 51,000 soldiers perished. Why so much death? Partly because the war began just as advances in technology allowed for deadlier guns and cannons. In addition to more lethal weapons, disease claimed up to two-thirds of all who perished in the Civil War. Sickness could cut troops down as surely as a burst of bullets.

But why was the Civil War fought? What was the issue at the heart of America's deadliest war?

A Pew Research survey from 2011, 150 years after the Civil War began, showed that 48 percent of the people who responded thought the Civil War was about "states' rights" compared to 38 percent who thought it was about slavery.[1] In saying that the war

---

1. Russell Heimlich, "What Caused the Civil War?", May 18, 2011, www.pewresearch .org/fact-tank/2011/05/18/what-caused-the-civil-war/.

was about states' rights, people mean that the Confederate states in the South did not go to war with the Union because they wanted to keep slavery but because they didn't like the federal government putting their nose into state-level matters. But if the war was about states' rights, then we have to ask, "What did the states want the right to do?" To answer this, let's look at the original documents from the states themselves.

South Carolina led the way as the first state to secede—or break off—from the Union. In their "Declaration of the Immediate Causes Which Induce and Justify the Secession of South Carolina from the Federal Union," the state listed as their reason the northern states' increasing antislavery attitudes, particularly their unwillingness to return enslaved people who had escaped to their former masters. "But an increasing hostility on the part of the non-slaveholding States to the institution of slavery, has led to a disregard of their obligations. . . . Thus the constituted compact has been deliberately broken and disregarded by the non-slaveholding States, and the consequence follows that South Carolina is released from her obligation."

Similarly, the Mississippi Articles of Secession explain the reasons why the state's leaders decided to withdraw from the Union and join the Confederacy, and they clearly tie their concerns to slavery. "Our position is thoroughly identified with the institution of slavery—the greatest material interest of the world. Its labor supplies the product which constitutes by far the largest and most important portions of commerce of the earth."

Confederate leaders themselves talked about the importance of slavery to their cause. Alexander Stephens, the vice president of the Confederate States of America, outlined the beliefs of the rebellious states. In his famous "Cornerstone Speech" given in March 1861, he said the Confederacy's "cornerstone rests upon the great truth, that the negro is not equal to the white man, that slavery—subordination to the superior race—is his natural and normal condition." Within the context of these sources, you could certainly say that Confederate states seceded for states' rights—but only if you mean the supposed right of states to decide whether they would allow white people to own Black people.

In the end, the Confederacy was defeated, the Union was preserved, and the immoral institution of slavery began to crumble with the Emancipation Proclamation issued on January 1, 1863. But that did not actually end slavery nationwide. Slavery was officially outlawed with the Thirteenth Amendment on January 31, 1865. It stated, "Neither slavery nor involuntary servitude, except as a punishment for crime whereof the party shall have been duly convicted, shall exist within the United States, or any place subject to their jurisdiction." But it still took several months to spread the word. Enslaved Black people in Texas didn't get the announcement until June 19, 1865, a day that became known as Juneteenth (which we'll learn more about in chapter 11).

Reconstruction

I love LEGO. I didn't play with them much as a kid, but I got into them as an adult. I build LEGO sets—Harry Potter, Star Wars, even Trolls—to relax and unwind. One time I had just finished building a really complicated LEGO set, and I left it on the dining room table where I had been building it. When I came back a few hours later, it was scattered in a hundred pieces across the floor. It turns out my ten-year-old son had been playing with it and dropped it. I was so frustrated! All that work only to have it destroyed. If someone can get that upset over a broken LEGO set, imagine how angry Black people felt when so much of the hard work they put into winning their freedom was destroyed after the Civil War.

As the chaos of the Civil War ended, African Americans turned their faces toward the warm dawn of freedom. For a brief, breathless moment it seemed as if the nation might finally live up to its guarantees of life, liberty, and the pursuit of happiness for everyone. That feeling of hope lasted only a moment before it was snatched away.

No other period of American history held as much hope for Black equality as the time of Reconstruction following the Civil War. Race-based chattel slavery was over. Few events in the history of the country could compare in terms of importance. And efforts to eliminate racism and create equity between different racial groups could have continued. Life could have been made more fair for women (who couldn't vote yet), Native Americans (who were victims of sickness and violence as the United States expanded and stole their lands), and the poor (who needed the opportunity to get out of their current conditions). While some significant reforms did happen, powerful forces stepped in to re-create a racial system where white men were at the top of society and everyone else was not.

For ten years or so after the Civil War, the newly freed Black population eagerly entered into the civic life of the nation. They ran for political office, opened businesses, started schools, and grasped for the American dream for the first time.

In 1865, President Abraham Lincoln set up the Bureau of Refugees, Freedmen, and Abandoned Lands, typically known as the Freedmen's Bureau. This government program was responsible for providing food and clothing to formerly enslaved people, helping them find family members who had been sold to other plantation owners, assisting the jobless in finding employment, setting up hospitals and schools (including colleges like Clark Atlanta and Howard University), and partnering with Black people as they adjusted to life as free people.

Although the Freedmen's Bureau didn't have as much money as it needed to do the job well—and the resources it did have were sometimes used in questionable ways—the fact that it existed at all was a big deal. It proved that some lawmakers believed the federal government had a duty to help those it had formerly allowed to be enslaved.

This era saw a blossoming of Black political participation. While many whites assumed that Black people didn't have the brains or common sense needed to participate in a democracy, Black leaders quickly proved them wrong.

Hiram Revels became the first Black US Senator in the nation's history. P. B. S. Pinchback served for a short time as the governor of Louisiana, the first Black person ever to serve in the highest political office in the state. During Reconstruction, eight hundred Black men gained office in state legislatures as politicians who wrote laws for their states.

Remember how Frederick Douglass wasn't allowed to read? Now Black people hustled to take advantage of their freedom by going to school. Freed people worked hard at getting an education. Since many Black people had been denied the right to learn everything white kids learned, they eagerly started public schools to learn their "letters and figures."

One of the main reasons Black people showed so much enthusiasm about reading was because they were finally able to read the Bible for themselves. On the rare occasions when

Black people were allowed to hear white preachers, the sermons preached often encouraged the Black listeners to be more obedient to their heavenly and earthly masters. Rarely did they hear that God loved all people equally.

While the federal government stepped in to enforce the civil rights of its Black residents by officially ending slavery, making freed slaves into US citizens, and allowing Black men to vote, the promise of equality shone brightly. But the presidential election of 1876 changed everything.

Jim Crow & The Great Migration

It started with the "Compromise of 1877." In a hotly contested election, Democrats agreed to make Rutherford B. Hayes president as long as he allowed the Southern states to make their own decisions when it came to civil rights. Before this, government soldiers had been ordered to stay in the South and make sure people followed the new rules that said Black people should be treated the same as white people. But in 1877, Hayes ordered those soldiers to leave the South. This meant that Black citizens could no longer count on the government to enforce their civil rights. They were left to face the terrorism of white supremacists on their own.

Things quickly got worse for Black people in the South. The southern states began writing segregation laws, known as "Jim Crow" laws. The name Jim Crow came from a comedy routine that wasn't actually funny, where a white person would paint their face black and make fun of Black people based on stereotypes. (By the way, it's not funny to paint your face and dress up as a person of a different race for Halloween. This makes another people group or culture into an unfunny joke.) As a result, Jim Crow became a disrespectful name for African Americans across the South.

Although you may not have heard the term "Jim Crow," you probably have heard that for a long time white people and Black people were separated by race—in churches, on buses, in movie theaters, schools, restaurants, and more. Separating people based on race is called segregation. Did you ever wonder why Black and white people were segregated? Legally speaking, it started with a single court case.

In 1891, the Louisiana government passed a law to force Black people to ride in separate rail cars from whites when they were on trains. The next year, Black citizens and some lawmakers wanted to show how silly and wrong that rule was. They asked Homer A. Plessy, who was one-eighth Black, to test the new law by riding in the "white" car. People sometimes thought Plessy was white instead of Black, because he had very light skin, so the lawmakers were hoping Plessy would be able to ride in the white car without anyone noticing.

Someone told the railroad company about Plessy's identity, however, and the railway arrested Plessy after he refused to move to the "colored" car. Lawyers for Plessy argued that Louisiana's law treated people unfairly based on the color of their skin. The case went all the way to the Supreme Court, and on May 18, 1896, the justices ruled that Plessy's rights had not been violated. They said that just because people were treated differently, it didn't mean that one of them was inferior to the other.

The *Plessy v. Ferguson* decision legalized what soon became standard practice throughout the country for the next sixty years—the "separate but equal" doctrine, or segregation. Maybe that doesn't sound like a big deal, because equal is supposed to be equal, no matter how separate, right? But that's not how it works in real life.

Imagine this scenario: Someone in your class had a birthday and brought in donuts to share. The donut box is filled with a wide variety of options. There are chocolate donuts with sprinkles, glazed donuts, creme-filled donuts, custard-filled donuts, and plain donuts. Your teacher is tall and his son, who happens to be in the class, is tall too. The class is told to line up by height order to grab a donut from the box. The tallest kids in class go first and can choose from any donut they want. The shortest kids can only choose the donuts no one else wanted . . . if there are any left! Even if you got a donut, it wasn't exactly fair or equal.

Now imagine that it isn't donuts we're talking about. Maybe it's a job, a college education, or buying a house that is at stake. Since white people are in charge of how society is organized, they have a way of making the rules so they always get the best options and opportunities. Maybe this isn't always intentional, but the results are usually the same.

The "separate but equal" doctrine made it possible for southern states to create different schools, different public drinking fountains, and different access to businesses for people based on the color of their skin.

> **Nationalism:** The belief that the country where you live is the best country in the world and that people coming in from other countries will make things worse in some way

This era also saw the rise of white supremacist organizations like the Ku Klux Klan (or KKK). The Klan launched immediately after the end of the Civil War with the goal of keeping whites in power. Their methods were full of threats and violence.

Over the years, the KKK blended Christianity, **nationalism**, and white supremacy into a toxic recipe for hate. To make sure their version of a white, Christian society stayed in control, the KKK wasn't afraid to lynch people, or intimidate them with threats or actual violence in order to keep "undesirable" people in their place.

Although white supremacy wasn't limited to the former Confederate states, it still seemed better for many Black folks to live anywhere other than the Jim Crow South. This led to a huge number of Black people moving from the South to cities in the North, Midwest, and East and West Coasts, which is referred to as the Great Migration. This is why I grew up near Chicago. Most of my grandparents had been born in the South, including Louisiana and Mississippi. But at some point they made their way North to create a better life for themselves in places they thought had less racism.

Some major cities saw their Black populations more than double between 1920 and 1930. Chicago's Black population grew from 109,500 to 234,000, New York City's from 152,000 to 328,000, and Detroit's from 41,000 to 120,066.[2] As so many Black people moved into these cities, white people began to see city living differently.

As tensions rose between the incoming Black families and their white neighbors, some white people moved out of the cities and into surrounding communities called suburbs. As they moved, real estate companies and government officials set up rules about where Black people were and were not able to live. This is part of why Black people, white people, and other people of color to this day live in neighborhoods separated from one another.

---

2. Glenda E. Gilmore and Thomas J. Sugrue, *These United States: A Nation in the Making, 1890 to the Present* (New York: Norton, 2015), 143.

While some Black people migrated in hopes of improving their circumstances, others stayed put and worked for change in their home communities. Unfortunately, for Black people living in the Jim Crow South, things would continue to get worse until a massive movement to gain equal rights as citizens of the United States.

CHAPTER 10

The History of Race in America: The Fight for Justice

The Civil Rights Movement

The Civil Rights movement of the 1950s and 1960s was a time of great change. As white soldiers returned home from serving overseas in World War II (WWII), many found new opportunities for advancement through college educations, affordable houses, and good-paying jobs. As Black soldiers returned home, they were denied many of the same opportunities. They had left their families, defended their nation, and risked their lives just as white soldiers did, but at home they were denied their basic rights.

The states that had Jim Crow laws in effect made it nearly impossible for Black people to get ahead in society. But even in the North, new and affordable housing communities were closed off to Black people. The "separate but equal" doctrine was proving to be anything but equal in many areas of post-WWII America.

We've already seen how Emmett Till's death brought

different Civil Rights organizations together, but there was another child who helped launch the movement into action: Linda Brown.

Nine-year-old Linda Brown likely had no idea that she would be part of a group of Black families who would overturn the nearly sixty-year-old *Plessy v. Ferguson* decision and the nation's legal commitment to segregation in public facilities. In 1951, Linda's father simply did not want his little girl to have to cross railroad yards and a busy street to get to a school that couldn't compare to the white schools in Topeka, Kansas. Sumner Elementary School was much closer to the Brown home and had a better building, better-trained teachers, and more funding for its programs. It also happened to be all-white. When the school's officials refused to let Linda attend there, her dad joined with four other cases in the now-famous *Brown v. Board of Education of Topeka*.

In explaining the Supreme Court's unanimous decision—a situation where everyone agrees on an issue and votes the same way—Chief Justice Earl Warren wrote, "We conclude that, in the field of public education, the doctrine of 'separate but equal' has no place. Separate educational facilities are inherently unequal."[1]

The Supreme Court decision struck the South like a bolt of lightning. The law may have been changed in Washington D.C., but it would require local law enforcement to support it. For southern states who still saw segregation as the natural—or even the "Christian"—way of life, significant changes toward equity would only be achieved with significant sacrifice.

This era saw Dr. Martin Luther King Jr. engaged in

---

1. "Transcript of Brown v. Board of Education (1954)," ourdocuments.gov, www.ourdocuments.gov/doc.php?flash=false&doc=87&page=transcript.

peaceful protests against the unfair laws across the South. It included Rosa Parks refusing to give up her bus seat to a white passenger. It featured the Freedom Riders, who took bus trips throughout the South, refusing to bow to the segregation laws that made whites and Blacks sit in different places, and not giving up even when buses were bombed and riders were beaten for their stand against injustice.

The names of John Lewis, Malcolm X, Diane Nash, James Farmer, Bayard Rustin, Roy Wilkins, A. Philip Randolph, Whitney Young, and Fannie Lou Hamer became well-known. Each person stood up against an unjust system and sacrificed their time, their comfort, and sometimes their lives to move society toward freedom for all.

There are more stories worthy of your time than can be written down in this brief overview, and we'll visit a few throughout the book, but for now let's look at the next era.

The Twentieth Century to Now

By 1970, women and men of African descent had come a long way in a society where they started out as property. With the passage of the Civil Rights Act of 1964 and the Voting Rights legislation of 1965, Black people had more opportunities for advancement than they had ever had before, but they were still a far cry from the position in society white people were born into.

No amount of legislation can change a person's heart to accept others. Heart-changing power is God's alone. Still, legislation is an important step toward encouraging members of society to treat each other fairly. Unfortunately, in the years which followed the Civil Rights movement, government forces used the public's fear of change to pass new laws that unfairly targeted Black citizens and people of color.

Imagine your school principal makes a new rule that any student found with candy will not just be warned or given some minor punishment, they will be suspended. If that same student gets caught with candy once or twice more, they will be expelled. Now imagine that the principal sends monitors out into the school to check for kids with candy, but the monitors only look into one or two classrooms. The kids in that classroom might not bring candy more often than students in other classes, but because the monitors are paying more attention to those one or two classes, more students there get suspended or expelled. That's sort of how policing works in the United States.

Law-and-order politics promises stability by promoting an increasingly aggressive stance toward criminal justice. Basically, the government promises to get criminals off the streets. Then, when it looks for criminals to lock up, law enforcement officers primarily look in big cities and poor communities where Black people and other people of color are more likely to be found.

Law-and-order politics: A strategy where politicians promise to be tough on crime in the name of protecting citizens, which can result in brutal policing tactics and unfair prison sentences for minor crimes

Racial discrimination happens everywhere. Many times, it happens without people even thinking about it. One of the hidden factors behind this could be how people are naturally afraid of others who don't look like them. This fear's fancy name is *xenophobia* (pronounced zee-no-fo-bee-uh), and it specifically refers to a fear or hatred of people who are thought to be foreign or strange. When a white person looks at a Black person as being too different from them, the fear they feel can make the Black person seem more threatening than they actually are.

On February 26, 2012, a Black seventeen-year-old high school student named Trayvon Martin was walking back to his father's fiancée's townhouse, a place he had visited several times before, in a gated community of Sanford, Florida. He wore a hoodie sweatshirt and had Skittles and an iced tea in his hand. George Zimmerman, a Hispanic and multiracial man patrolling on neighborhood watch, was driving by and called the police to report Martin as a suspicious person. A written account of the call reports him as saying, "We've had some break-ins in my neighborhood, and there's a real suspicious guy." At some point, Martin started running. Zimmerman chased him, even though the police dispatcher—the person responsible for sending police assistance to a certain location—told him it wasn't necessary. Zimmerman can be heard swearing and saying, "They always get away."

What happened next remains a mystery because only one person remains alive to tell the story. Somehow, Zimmerman and Martin got into a fight. Zimmerman, who legally owned a gun, shot Martin once in the chest. Zimmerman phoned police at 7:09 p.m., and paramedics pronounced Martin dead at 7:30 p.m. In just a few minutes, a normal walk to the local convenience store for snacks had resulted in Trayvon's murder.

On July 13, 2013, George Zimmerman was declared to be not guilty in the murder of Trayvon Martin.

That same day, Alicia Garza, a Black activist and writer in Oakland, California, sat down at her computer to write what she called "a love letter to black people." In the short post, she wrote, "Black people. I love you. I love us. Our lives matter." Her friend and fellow activist, Patrisse Cullors, responded to the post with the words, "Declaration: black bodies will no longer be sacrificed for the rest of the world's enlightenment. i am done. i am so done. trayvon, you are loved infinitely. #blacklivesmatter." Together with their friend Opal Tometi, these three Black women started a hashtag that flowered into a movement that would significantly change the conversation about race and justice in America.[2]

The #BlackLivesMatter hashtag started in response to the murder of Trayvon Martin, but it became well-known in 2014 with the murder of Mike Brown, a teenager from Ferguson, Missouri.

Mike Brown and a friend were walking in the middle of a two-lane street when a police officer named Darren Wilson drove by and told them to use the sidewalk. Words were exchanged, the situation escalated, and the white officer and Brown ended up scuffling. The officer shot and killed Brown, who was unarmed at the time of his death.

After an unusual court process, District Attorney Robert P. McCulloch announced that Officer Wilson wouldn't face criminal charges for the shooting.

Black people and their allies across the nation responded in outrage. Protestors took to the streets in more than 150 cities. The reality that yet another unarmed Black youth had been killed and no one would face legal penalties sent a message that Black lives could be ended and no one would be held responsible.

Observers saw a pattern in the deaths of Trayvon Martin and Mike Brown that looked a lot like the unlimited power of life and death slaveholders had held over enslaved Blacks and

---

2. Linda Steiner and Silvio Waisbord, eds., *News of Baltimore: Race, Rage and the City* (New York: Rutledge, 2017), 123.

the decades of lynchings that went unpunished during the Jim Crow era. Even in the past few years, the list of Black human beings who have become hashtags has grown ever longer—Stephon Clark, Philando Castile, Freddie Gray, Walter Scott, Jamar Clark, Rekia Boyd, Eric Garner, Sandra Bland, Tamir Rice, George Floyd, and Breonna Taylor, to name just a few. **Activists** have used the phrase *Black lives matter* because the number of killings have sent the message that Black lives do not, in fact, matter.

Activists: People who are actively committed to changing society to become more just

This is the age we are in right now. Racism is still alive. Prejudice and fear are still working against bringing people together. But understanding the history of racism in America is an important first step to becoming aware enough to stop it in the future.

CHAPTER 11

Racial Justice in Action: Uncovering History

Understanding how racism runs throughout the history of this country will help you know what you are fighting against. In this chapter, you'll discover some tips for interacting with history wisely: learning from it, commemorating it, and recognizing how the past connects to the present.

How to Spot Trustworthy History

Have you ever told a story and exaggerated just a bit to make it seem like you were faster, smarter, funnier, or more heroic? We all do it because we all like to make ourselves look good. We do the same thing with history. Some people like to tell a version of history to make their favorite hero or nation look good. But doing that means you play with the facts or even tell outright lies. Just like you can't believe everything everyone says, just because someone calls it "history" doesn't mean that you can automatically believe what they say. You have to do your homework and make sure what they say is true.

History, even when it is written in books like this, is more than just a gathering of facts. The facts require interpretation and opinion. What topics people choose, what questions they ask, what access they have to resources, how they choose to arrange the facts, and what meaning they give to historical events all depend on how someone is influenced by their personal feelings, tastes, or opinions.

This isn't necessarily a bad thing as long as you know history-telling has some sort of **bias**. But if all history has some sort of slant and is subject to error, then how do you know which history to trust? And since what is true for history sources is also true for social media posts, maybe we should be asking, how do you know what things (history *or* social media) you can trust?

Bias: A tendency to be for or against something based on personal interpretation and not just facts

The first step is knowing which questions to ask:

- Who wrote this? Can you be sure they actually wrote or said it?
- Who was this written or said to?
- Who might benefit or be harmed by this information?
- What might have been left out of this information? Are there other sources saying different things?
- Why do you think this is true or untrue?

Every historian knows you should check into something for yourself before you can be sure it is true. It's important to know what things are trustworthy and who might benefit from people believing something, whether it is true or not. Make sure you check with more than one source before you accept whether something is real.

You also need to be on the lookout for historical accounts

that tell the story of humanity as one with clear heroes and villains. Real life isn't like a Marvel Comics movie. There's usually not a clear "bad guy," like Thanos, who clearly commits evil actions. There's not an obvious "good guy," like Captain America, who always does the right thing. Overly simple stories that pit champions of progress against backward-thinking and morally questionable opponents usually hide more than they reveal. Was victory in World War II a triumph? Not according to the victims of the atomic bombs dropped on Hiroshima and Nagasaki or those who feared nuclear war. Were the cowboys the "good guys" and the Native Americans the "bad guys"? Not if you view it from the perspective of the indigenous inhabitants.

Where we find ourselves in the present day is not a neat story. The "good" people can do bad things. And the "bad" people even sometimes do the right thing. The line between good and evil is not always clear. Search for the histories that honor the complexity of the human experience.

Learn Your Local History

One of the best places to learn about the history of race is right where you are. Important history is all around us, but the significance of what happened nearby can sometimes be lost because sometimes we grow so used to seeing our surroundings that we have to rediscover how to look deeply at them to learn lessons from the local past.

Have you ever wondered who or what a place was named after? Names surround us—on street signs, buildings, counties, and cities. Names matter. They explain part of a community's history, who gets to tell that history, and what they value. The names in your community communicate a lot about its history.

Names like Arapahoe County, Missisquoi River, and Mohegan Elementary School reveal a hard truth about cities across the United States. From the most populous cities on the coasts to the rolling prairies of the heartland, Native Americans were here first, and we are on their land, which we stole.

As people concerned about racial justice grapple with the contradiction of living in the "Land of Liberty" that was built on the displacement and murder of Native Americans, one proactive measure we can take is to learn who the original inhabitants were and where they are now.

Several tools now exist to remind us of who originally lived on the land we currently occupy. There are interactive maps online that allow you to enter an address or a zip code, which then tell you which indigenous nations originally lived on the land in that area. Beyond simply knowing the name of the nation, you can go further by learning its history. What language did they speak? What treaties or wars led to their displacement? What is the state of the nation in the present day?

Conduct an Oral History

On July 17, 2020, two leaders of the Civil Rights movement both died. Congressman John Lewis had been fighting for racial justice since the 1960s on the streets and in the nation's capital, and Rev. C. T. Vivian was one of the Freedom Riders who worked to end segregation and spent his life preaching and organizing for racial progress. Today, the people who participated in the Civil Rights movement are in the final years of their lives. Even the youngest of these women and men are now in their seventies and eighties. What will happen when this last generation of eyewitnesses passes from the earth?

What questions will remain unanswered? Who will inspire the next generation of racial justice activists?

We cannot extend anyone's life forever, but we can honor their stories by inviting them to retell and record those narratives. This is the purpose of oral history. *Oral* means "spoken," and the Oral History Association says oral history is "a method of gathering, preserving, and interpreting the voices and memories of people, communities, and participants in past events."[1]

If you've ever asked an older person to tell you a real story about their life or memories, you've taken the first step in doing an oral history. Before human beings created written language, they passed down stories of their families and communities through oral histories. In West African tradition, the griot (pronounced *GREE-o*) was a person responsible for remembering and sharing stories. They would communicate through poetry and song, and their role was incredibly important in preserving the history and heritage of a people. We need modern-day griots who will take the responsibility to record and share the oral recollections of people.

To see and hear some examples, the Library of Congress has a large collection of oral history projects that are digitized and searchable.

Go ahead. Ask your parents, grandparents, or trusted family friends to tell their stories. You can make it fun. Record their voices with the voice memo app on a phone. Or you can even record a video of them talking.

Just remember, your efforts to discover oral histories should be collected and recorded thoughtfully. Oral history is first and foremost a way of showing honor. You must honor the people behind the stories. At the most basic level, taking

---

1. Visit oralhistory.org for extensive resources and training materials for doing oral history.

an oral history means you cannot share anyone's story without their express permission. Even if it is only meant for your own personal use, you must tell the person why you are asking them to share their very personal stories and memories.

First, figure out what you want to know. An oral history isn't just "shooting the breeze." Oral history is talking on purpose. You want to find out specific information. The best way to make sure you conduct a good oral history interview is to plan out your questions beforehand. When possible, send the questions to the person ahead of the interview so they have time to think and even collect some relevant artifacts. Ask questions that don't have a simple yes or no answer. For example:

- What was school like growing up?
- What was your first job?
- Can you describe the racial climate where you grew up?
- Did you grow up in a religious community? What did the people around you communicate about race?
- Do any incidents around race stand out to you?

A resource from the University of California at Los Angeles (UCLA) advises, "In general, think of the various topics of your interview as structured like an inverted pyramid: broad, general questions first, followed by follow-up questions that ask for more detail."[2] The goal is to collect stories to better understand the historical context of a community through the eyes of a particular person. These histories can add much-needed information that you cannot find online or in books, and they will round out other facts and data.

---

2. "Interviewing Guidelines," www.library.ucla.edu/location/library-special-collections /location/center-oral-history-research/resources/interviewing-guidelines.

Go to a Museum

When he was eight, I took my son to the National Civil Rights Museum in Memphis. It is built into the Lorraine Motel, which is where Martin Luther King Jr. was shot. My son really wasn't into it. He kept rushing me through the museum. But when we stood outside of the museum building, we looked up to the balcony at the exact spot where King had been standing when the bullet struck. We both stood there silently.

On the way home, he started asking lots of questions about King, and the Civil Rights movement, and race. He's probably forgotten most of the visit, but he will always remember that moment standing outside and looking up at the balcony where King stood.

I know going to museums may seem like it's something you only do when an adult makes you, but you can learn a lot about racial history. Find out what museums around you focus on underrepresented people, such as Black history or Native American history. Go there and read—*really read*—the displays. Maybe see if there's a program they put on for students and make plans to watch it. You could even suggest it to your teacher and be part of the planning when your class takes a trip. Museums are built for learning. Take advantage of them as you build your awareness around race.

Learn How to Commemorate Juneteenth

In the days before the internet and email, news tended to travel slowly. It wasn't until June 19, 1865—a full two months after Robert E. Lee surrendered his Confederate Army to Union forces and two years after the Emancipation Proclamation—that enslaved Black people in Texas heard that the Civil War had ended and that their emancipation would soon be a reality. In the wake of the announcement, Black people erupted into celebration. The long night of their enslavement was finally giving way to the bright dawn of freedom.

Juneteenth, which is a mash-up of the words *June* and *nineteenth*, stands as the oldest celebration of Black emancipation in the United States. To the Black community, the occasion has long marked the progress of the United States from legally approving race-based chattel slavery to legally abolishing it after centuries of resistance, the initiation of the nation's bloodiest war, and a constitutional amendment. Historically speaking, few events compare to the significance of the abolition of slavery in the United States. It forever changed the political and social landscape of the country. And on June 17, 2021—as I was writing this book—Juneteenth was signed into law as a federal holiday for all American people to commemorate.

But how should you go about celebrating this important day? The first thing to keep in mind is that white people should be careful not to **appropriate** the holiday from Black people. This happens when white people erase the suffering and brutality of slavery in favor of a celebratory message of ongoing progress. It also happens when white people fail to remember their historic role in racial injustice and celebrate as if they had nothing to do with the conditions that made Black emancipation necessary in the first place. The fact remains that white people practiced and defended race-based chattel slavery in the United States, and this should be a cause for humble sorrow. While it is a day of celebration for Black people, white people

Appropriate: To take and use elements of a different culture without understanding or respecting it

must rejoice along with Black people while also remembering the white supremacy their ancestors created and from which they still benefit.

With all that in mind, here are some activities you could take part in that focus on remembering America's past as well as what has been accomplished since the end of the Civil War—while also looking at what can be done to continue the fight for equity and racial justice today.

- To help educate you further on Juneteenth, go to your local library or bookstore and pick up several books on the history of the holiday that you can read and discuss with others.
- Attend a Juneteenth event in person or online. If you can, talk to Black attendees about why the event is important to them so it can help your own understanding.
- Gather friends and family members to celebrate. Enjoy being together, but also take time to discuss America's past and if needed help others understand why recognizing that history is so important.
- Donate a part of your allowance to a racial justice cause or make a point of visiting a Black-owned business to help support the community around you. (And these are great things to do year-round as well!)

Watch, Read, or Listen to the News

When I was a junior high student, every morning, my homeroom teacher would turn on this kid news program on television. It was only about five minutes long, but it gave important news from around the country and around the world. I loved hearing about places and people far away and having a sense that I was "in the know" about events.

Paying attention to the news is a great way to learn about what is going on with race today. You can learn about police reforms, state and national elections, the battle for voting rights, and victories that activists have won. There are some good news outlets made specifically for kids such as *Scholastic Kids Press*, the *Smithsonian's Tween Tribune*, and *The Learning Network* by the *New York Times*.

The news is not just for adults. If you want to fight racism, you have to know what's going on, so keep up with current events. One great way to do that is by reading, watching, or listening to the news.

Questions to Consider

- What facts were you surprised to learn about the history of racism in America?
- Who is someone you read about that you would like to further research?
- Who could you conduct an oral history with? What questions will you ask them?
- What are some ways you can commemorate Juneteenth?
- What books by Black authors or about Black history will you add to your reading list?

Kamala Harris's Journey & Faith

Vice President Kamala Harris is second-in-command when it comes to running the country, but she is first in many ways. The Honorable Ms. Harris is the first woman, first daughter of immigrants, and first woman of color to hold the office of vice president. To be specific, Vice President Harris is the first Black and South Asian (from India) person to serve in her current role.

Many have compared her political rise to former president Barack Obama, whose multiracial identity as the son of a Black father and a white mother was a big deal to some people. Vice President Harris sees why people would make the comparison, but she'd rather they didn't. She wants to be judged by her personal actions instead of how others see her.

"So much so," Vice President Harris told *The Washington Post* in February 2019, "that when I first ran for office that was one of the things that I struggled with, which is that you are forced through that process to define yourself in a way that you fit neatly into the compartment that other people have created.

"My point was: I am who I am. I'm good with it. You might need to figure it out, but I'm fine with it."[1]

This comfort level with her racial identity is part of how she was raised. Her mother, Shyamala Gopalan, was active in the Civil Rights movement in California in the 1960s and 1970s, bringing Harris along on marches in a stroller. Although Gopalan immigrated to America from Chennai in southeast India, she knew her kids—Kamala and her sister, Maya—would be seen through the American lens of race as Black.

"My mother understood very well that she was raising two black daughters," wrote Vice President Harris in her book, *The Truths We Hold.* "She was determined to make sure we would grow into confident, proud black women."[2]

Part of this journey toward confidence can be traced back to her faith. In an email interview with *Religion News Service,* Vice President Harris wrote, "On Sundays, my mother would dress my sister, Maya, and me in our Sunday best and send us off to the 23rd Avenue Church of God in Oakland, California, where Maya and I sang in the children's choir. That's where I formed some of my earliest memories of the Bible's teachings. It's where I learned that 'faith' is a verb, and that we must live it, and show it, in action."

Her conviction to live out her faith can be seen throughout her career as she has sought to amplify the voices of those society has chosen not to hear. "The God I have always believed in

---

1. Kevin Sullivan, "'I Am Who I Am': Kamala Harris, Daughter of Indian and Jamaican Immigrants, Defines Herself Simply as 'American'," *The Washington Post,* February 2, 2019, www.washingtonpost.com/politics/i-am-who-i-am-kamala-harris-daughter-of -indian-and-jamaican-immigrants-defines-herself-simply-as-american/2019/02/02 /0b278536–24b7–11e9-ad53–824486280311_story.html.
2. Kamala Harris, *The Truths We Hold: An American Journey* (New York: Penguin Press, 2019), 10.

is a loving God, a God who asks us to serve others and speak up for others, especially those who are not wealthy or powerful and cannot speak up for themselves," she wrote in the same article. "I can trace my belief in the importance of public service back to learning the parable of the good Samaritan and other biblical teachings about looking out for our neighbors—and understanding that our neighbors aren't just those who live in our ZIP code, but include the stranger, too."[3]

Being able to identify with the disinherited is an important part of what it means to be a follower of Jesus. Romans 12:15–16 says, "Rejoice with those who rejoice; mourn with those who mourn. Live in harmony with one another. Do not be proud, but be willing to associate with people of low position. Do not be conceited."

When asked by *The Washington Post* about how her upbringing as a Black American has shaped her as a person, the vice president said, "It's kind of like asking how did eating food shape who I am today.

"It affects everything about who I am. Growing up as a black person in America made me aware of certain things that, maybe if you didn't grow up black in America, you wouldn't be aware of."

Asked for an example, she said, "Racism."

To explain, she said, "I grew up in a hot spot of the civil rights movement. But that civil rights movement involved blacks, it involved Jews, it involved Asians, it involved Chicanos, it involved a multitude of people who were aware that there were laws that were not equally applied to all people."[4]

---

3. Maina Mwaura, "Kamala Harris Talks About Her Own Faith," Religion News Service, January 27, 2021, https://ifyc.org/article/kamala-harris-talks-about-her-own-faith.
4. Sullivan, "'I Am Who I Am,'" *Washington Post*.

Black Christians and other oppressed people often find solidarity with those working for justice, as Vice President Kamala Harris has done. And though Christianity itself is supposed to bring people together in love, we live in a world where Black Christians who stand against police brutality under the banner of #BlackLivesMatter are dismissed as radicals by white Christians who justify such police tactics as necessary to keeping the peace.

Jesus said in John 13:34–35, "A new commandment I give to you, that you love one another: just as I have loved you, you also are to love one another. By this all people will know that you are my disciples, if you have love for one another"(ESV).

As Christians wrestle with this call to love one another, to see God's image in each other, it is important to search our own lives, our understandings of ourselves, our histories, and our racial self-awareness to be able to see the world as God sees it. To love others as Jesus loves us is to see others as Jesus sees us.

So what do you see when you look in the mirror?

Questions to Consider

- Why might Vice President Kamala Harris feel pressured by society with regard to her race? Do you ever feel pressured to act or speak in certain ways because of your race?
- Using John 13:34-35 as your guide, what evidence in your life would let others know you are Christ's follower?

CHAPTER 12

How to Explore Your Racial Identity

In interviews and in her work, Vice President Harris seems completely comfortable with her racial identity. That level of comfort is possible for everyone, but it can only be achieved after we've done the work of growing our racial awareness. To discover a sense of one's race is called racial identity development, and this chapter explains the crucial need for people of all races to explore their racial identity and make sure they are moving toward greater self-awareness and sensitivity. You're never too young to pay attention to your racial identity development.

You're never too young to pay attention to your racial identity development.

What words would you use to describe yourself? A person's identity is made up of many different parts. There are visible pieces of your identity:

- What color is your skin?
- Are you a girl or a boy?

- How old are you?
- What kind of clothes do you wear?

And there are other pieces of your identity:

- What languages do you speak?
- Where in the world do you live?
- How big is your family?
- Where are you in the birth order of siblings?
- What do you believe about God?

All these factors make up your self-identity (how you see yourself), as well as your social identity (how other people see you). As you grow up, your understanding of your identity will change. What the people around you say and do will influence how you think and feel about yourself.

Since some aspects of your identity are more visible than others, you'll find that people tend to make a bigger deal of them. That includes your race and ethnicity. Sometimes people say we should be "colorblind." What they mean is that we should not pay attention to a person's race and just treat everyone the same.

Author Robin DiAngelo, in her book *White Fragility*, lists several statements that may mean a person has accepted the theory of colorblindness.

"I was taught to treat everyone the same."
"I don't care if you're pink, purple, or polka-dotted."
"Focusing on race is what divides us."[1]

Yet the theory of colorblindness denies the historic and

1. Robin DiAngelo, *White Fragility: Why It Is So Hard for White People to Talk About Racism* (Boston, MA: Beacon Press, 2020), 77, 79.

real ways that race affects people of color and shapes the thinking and behaviors of white people. The lens of colorblindness begins to crack for white people in the "encounter" phase, when they develop a personal relationship that forces them to confront the real-life differences that exist because of race. This phase may include a sense of discomfort, confusion, or guilt as the white person realizes her or his unearned advantages in a society that favors whiteness.

If the white person chooses to courageously continue down the path of racial awareness, color-blindness eventually gives way to color-consciousness.

The goal should not be to ignore our differences but to celebrate them as part of God's diverse image.

It's never good to be blind to a part of someone's identity. The goal should not be to ignore our differences but to celebrate them as part of God's diverse image.

One of the most complete guides to racial identity development comes from Dr. Beverly Daniel Tatum, a social psychologist and former college president. In 1997, she wrote a book called *Why Are All the Black Kids Sitting Together in the Cafeteria? And Other Conversations About Race.* The book proved to be so helpful that she wrote a revised and updated edition in 2017. In it, Tatum defines racial identity as "the meaning each of us has constructed or is constructing about what it means to be a White person or a person of color in a race-conscious society."[2]

Racial identity is not just for Black people and other people of color. White people have a racial identity that must be explored as well. Let's explore one model for looking at how

---

2. Beverly Daniel Tatum, *Why Are All the Black Kids Sitting Together in the Cafeteria, and Other Conversations About Race* (New York: Basic, 2017), 77.

Cross's Five-Stage Model of Racial Identity Development[1]	
Stage 1: Pre-Encounter	A person may not be aware of her or his race or ethnicity. If they think about it at all, they may not realize how it will affect their life. Example: Saying, "We're all just people."
Stage 2: Encounter	A person has an encounter or experience that causes them to think about how their race or ethnicity affects them. This could be either a positive or a negative experience. For most people of color, this experience is often a negative one where they feel the effects of racism for the first time. Sometimes, these effects are related to society's stereotypes about their race or ethnicity. Example: Realizing, "My color wasn't supposed to matter, but clearly it does matter to people after all."
Stage 3: Immersion	After the encounter, the person must explore what it means to belong to a specific race or ethnicity. This could include researching one's history, learning a language, or participating in cultural activities. It is important in this phase to be with others who share your experiences. Instead of seeing this as a form of self-segregation, Beverly Tatum points out that this practice is an important part of learning to cope as a member of a smaller group within a dominant culture. Example: Even though society tells you differently, you finally believe "Black is beautiful."
Stage 4: Internalization	At this phase, the person in question has developed a secure sense of racial identity and is comfortable socializing both within and outside of their racial group. Example: You confidently declare, "I am comfortable in the skin I'm in."

1. Source: William Cross, *Shades of Black: Diversity in African American Identity*, cited in Beverly Daniel Tatum, *Why Are All the Black Kids Sitting Together in the Cafeteria?* (New York: Basic, 1997), adapted and elaborated by Lisa Sung (2/2002)

Stage 5: Commitment	For people of color, this phase shows how motivated an individual is to bring awareness of their specific group's struggles to a larger group. For members of the dominant culture, this phase highlights an individual's motivation to advocate for people of color, even when it could affect them negatively.
	Example: "I can learn from anyone of any race or ethnicity."

people think through their status as a member of a certain race or ethnicity. Developed in 1971 by William Cross, this model has been used by different people to explain how identity changes over time.

One of the most valuable parts about learning the racial-ethnic-cultural identity model is that it helps us think about racial awareness as a process with different stages. The word *development* points to a process of change—racial identity changes over time. If you can find out which stage of racial-ethnic-cultural identity you are at right now, you can more intentionally move toward racial maturity and awareness.

In general, everyone starts out not knowing as much about racial dynamics. They just assume that what white people value and the way they do things is right. Hopefully, by learning about the history of racism in America, you have come to realize that things aren't meant to be this way, that white people are in power because the system has been set up to favor them, and that something must be done to set historic injustices right.

Knowing where you are in your own racial identity development can help you name the emotions you are feeling and can move you toward more mature levels of racial awareness.

At some point in life, most people have an encounter with

racism that shakes up their previous thinking. In the United States, some Native Americans may have been shaken by the protests against the construction of the Dakota Access Pipeline (#NoDAPL). People of Latin American descent have rallied to oppose family separation at the border between the United States and Mexico. For young Black people, the murders of George Floyd and Breonna Taylor have been change agents for racial awareness and activism.

Some white people can go their whole lives without ever having an encounter that causes them to think about race. This leads to a shallow relationship with an aspect of who they are. If they do think about race, they may question why it matters to other people when it seems so insignificant to them.

Maybe you've heard some white people say things like, "Everyone can succeed if they just work hard, so they have only themselves to blame," or "I don't know why these people keep playing the race card." Such statements reveal attitudes that justify the privileged position white people have as the dominant culture and show a lack of empathy for the struggles of people of color. Yes, success requires hard work, but failing to recognize that Black people have a different starting point makes it seem like they are to blame when their hard work doesn't put them ahead of their white friends.

After an encounter does happen, the next step is immersion. To immerse something means to plunge in. Imagine yourself on a diving board. You can see the water below, but you don't know what lies beneath. An encounter with race is kind of like being pushed off the diving board. Whether you wanted to dive in or not, suddenly you need to figure out how to swim in the topic of race and ethnicity.

Some people in the immersion phase are so uncomfortable

in the water, they don't want to dive very deep. These people will find the edge of the pool as quickly as possible and go back to acting how they did before their encounter.

But swimmers know that after the uncomfortable shock of hitting the water, your body adjusts. The immersion phase can be good. Discovering the history of race won't always be enjoyable, but you may come across inspirational stories about people who fought against racism (like you are learning to do!) and gain a new hero. This phase can be hard work, but the experience will make you a better swimmer and much more comfortable in the skin you're in.

After immersion comes internalization. This phase means recognizing how race affects your life. It doesn't mean you accept things the way they are, only that you know why they work the way they do. It means being able to speak comfortably within your own racial group and with other racial groups, not because you see them as the same but because you recognize their differences and appreciate them as such.

The final phase is commitment. People at this phase understand racism is a real problem and all people—not just the people who experience racism's negative effects—are responsible for being part of the solution. People of color actively take steps toward ensuring their rights are protected. White people in the commitment phase become allies and advocates for people of color. For every racial and ethnic group in this phase, we should be doing our best to recognize the ongoing importance of race in society. Race and ethnicity can influence where a person is likely to live and attend school, how much a person makes at their job later in life, even the quality of the healthcare they receive.

At the same time, race and ethnicity are not the only parts

of your identity. Someone who is actively going through their own racial identity development will always be aware that they are sons, daughters, family members, students, and believers. The goal for everyone is to have a positive view of their racial and ethnic identity, one that does not require them to fit in with or reject the dominant culture or experiences, and one that values the diversity of other people. Racially mature people will honestly say that not only is their race a factor in how they experience the world but also that identity is more than skin deep.

Questions to Consider

- How would you describe your identity to someone you've never met before? How do you think God would describe you?
- What stage do you think you are in on the Racial Identity Development chart?

CHAPTER 13

Racial Justice in Action: How to Understand Your Racial Identity

It's time to turn your awareness inward. Science, theology, and history are all important to understanding how racism has shaped society, but you need to find out how it has shaped you personally. Think hard, dig deep, and discover who you are, where you came from, and how to interact better with those you may have trouble relating to.

Write Your Racial Autobiography

You've already read about Frederick Douglass, but you may recognize the names of other Black women and men who wrote about their experiences under slavery: Sojourner Truth, Nat Turner, and Solomon Northup, to name a few. From the late 1700s until the early 1900s, the "slave narrative" was an important genre of literature where Black people could tell their own stories of oppression and how they pursued racial justice.

These accounts revealed the hardship that was common for the lives of many enslaved and formerly enslaved Black people. Northerners and white people who would otherwise only hear lies about slavery read slave narratives and got a picture of the injustice built into the "peculiar institution" of slavery. These autobiographical works prodded necessary conversations about racism and slavery and motivated a small number of people to work for the abolition of slavery.

In a similar way, telling your own story of race, whether as a member of a marginalized group or as a white person, can also create the kind of personal motivation needed for measurable change. One reason people struggle to talk productively about race is because they have not looked deeply into their own stories. A lack of awareness of your narrative around race will make it harder to find yourself on the racial identity development spectrum. You may not even be aware of the ways race has affected you or the **prejudices** you have.

Prejudices: Opinions, usually negative, about someone else that aren't based on truth

Writing a racial autobiography is one way to uncover experiences around race that have made you think and feel in certain ways. It's also a good way to learn lessons and get insights from those experiences. A racial autobiography is a self-reported account of your history with race, and it has two main purposes: to better understand your own story and to build empathy for others.

There are no set rules for writing down your racial autobiography, but here are a few suggestions that may prove helpful. First, do your best to actually write your story down, by hand or on a digital device. Writing your racial autobiography forces you to replay your racial record, perhaps for the first time. Writing down this story will dust off memories, similar to looking at old pictures from past birthdays and family gatherings. Writing also forces you to think carefully about your words and how you want to express your thoughts. As you decide how to describe your experiences in writing, you will develop clearer ideas about them. Don't get bogged down trying to craft a perfect story. Stick figures of thoughts can always be fleshed out later.

You may want to let close friends or family members read your racial autobiography . . . or not. Maybe you will publish it on a blog or even in a book someday. But you should not feel any pressure to share your story. Writing a racial autobiography is mainly for your development, and it will be useful whether anyone ever sees it or not.

To spur your thinking, ask yourself the following questions:

- What is my earliest memory of race?
- Have I had any negative experiences associated with my racial identity or that of someone else?
- When did I start becoming aware of race?
- Who has taught me the most about race and diversity?
- Can I describe the different stages of racial identity development I've gone through and what made me aware of each?
- What concerns me about my racial past?
- What encourages me about my racial past?
- Why do I "do" racial justice? Why do I care about racism and fighting against it?

You may not be able to answer every question right away. Move on to the next one, but remember to come back. Answers may come to you later. And it's natural when writing about your history of racial experiences to reflect on the future as well. What do you want to be true about yourself when it comes to race and racism? How can you actively fight racism today? What will you do differently in light of what you have done before?

Famed writer Joan Didion started writing down her life experiences at five years old. Reflecting as an adult on the habit of keeping notebooks in her book *Slouching Towards Bethlehem*, she said, "I think we are well advised to keep on nodding terms with the people we used to be, whether we find them attractive company or not." Writing a racial autobiography will be an emotional experience for many people. You may remember a distressing encounter you once had. You may recall how some family members understand race and wince at the memory. You may realize how a comment you made years ago could have come across as racist. Your old self may not be your best self. The record of our previous selves may not make "attractive company," but it is honest company.

Explore Your Family's Racial Identity

So much of who we are as individuals is shaped by the people we spend time with, especially family members.

Exploring your racial identity would be incomplete without also diving into your family's past and present views and experiences with race. To explore your family's racial identity, you will need to do some research and have some honest conversations. You will also need to prepare yourself spiritually and emotionally for what you might find. Not everyone in your family is on the same journey toward racial maturity as you. They haven't read the same books or had the same experiences as you. You might feel shocked, saddened, or angered when you learn your family's racial narrative.

In some cases, you may be encouraged as you realize how intentional parents or mentors have been in developing your racial awareness and fighting against racism. Perhaps you'll find helpful patterns in your life and experiences that you can teach others.

In many Black families and families of color, older generations (like grandparents) do not talk about the discrimination they faced. Doing so may bring up feelings of past hurts and shame that can be painful to relive. In some cases, family members may not want to talk about incidents of racism because they want to shield others in their family from feeling the same pain they endured. In white families, there may also be feelings of guilt or shame associated with what racist family members did or believed. Yet unearthing these stories, with proper sensitivity and care, is essential to understanding your racial identity.

You could start by asking to look through old family photos. Try to identify who is in each picture. Do you know where they lived and in what time period the photo was taken? Did they immigrate to the country? From where?

You may consider talking to siblings or aunts and uncles about race or racist attitudes in your family. They may remember incidents or feelings that you do not, and their knowledge can round out your recollections. Parents, grandparents, and other relatives should also be consulted, but bear in mind that they may not want to talk about these things.

Be honest about your purpose. Tell people that you are trying to understand your racial history and identity better, and to do that you want to understand how the people who influenced you think about such topics. The goal is to gather information, not necessarily to tell them what you think.

Ask open-ended questions such as, "What was it like growing up in your family?" or "What do you remember about what was happening in your town when you were a teenager?" Listen without offering your own thoughts or judgments. Even if you find the stories hard to listen to, your willingness to listen will encourage more conversation.

In discovering your family's racial background, you will learn more about what you believe about race and why. You will more easily see how communities can contribute to help-ful or harmful ideas about race. And you will become more aware of how you can encourage those closest to you to take intentional steps toward racial justice.

Learn Another Language

In high school, Spanish classes were always some of my favorites. I *really* loved learning about the different foods from Spanish-speaking countries. One time our teacher brought in flan—a sweet custard with a layer of caramel on top—for the class to taste. A class with food involved? Sign me up!

I didn't realize it at the time, but learning another language was also about learning another culture. We talked about the history, experiences, and celebrations of other countries. It built in me an appreciation for differences and an interest in the world that I might not have gained until much later.

So learn another language! Just pick whatever is available and seems interesting to you. It takes a ton of practice to speak a different language well, but it's worth the effort. You'll be able to communicate with a whole other group of people. By the way, if you ever have a chance to study abroad—spending a semester or a year taking classes in a different country—do it!

Questions to Consider

- Whose autobiography would you most like to read?
- What is the most interesting part of your autobiography?
- Why do you think older generations are less likely to talk about their past experiences with racism? How can you listen in such a way to make them more comfortable?
- What other language would you most like to learn? What might it teach you about the people who speak it?

PART 2:
RELATIONSHIPS

Ruby's Fight

Six years after the US Supreme Court issued its ruling in *Brown v. Board of Education of Topeka*, segregated schools were still going strong in the state of Louisiana. In order to shift the blame from officials—who had the power to enforce desegregation—to students themselves, city officials in New Orleans, Louisiana, gave 150 Black kindergarteners an entrance exam designed to be so difficult that the children would fail. If they could say Black kids weren't smart enough to attend all-white schools, city officials could say it wasn't segregation that was the problem but the children themselves. Of course, white students were not required to take these entrance exams, and if they had been, most would likely have failed too.

Of the 150 Black kindergarteners who took the ridiculously hard exam, only six passed. Ruby Bridges was one of them.

"Everybody was coming over and congratulating my parents. 'She's so smart. She passed. We're so proud of her.' So, I actually thought that I was so smart that I passed this test that would allow me to go from first grade to college," Ruby recalled in an interview with CBN.[1]

---

1. Quotes throughout this section are taken from the interview "Ruby Bridges Shares the Key to Overcoming Racism," www1.cbn.com/ruby-bridges-shares-key-overcoming-racism.

Ruby was selected to attend the all-white William Frantz Elementary School. She was supposed to be going with two other Black girls who passed the entrance exam, but before their first day the other two girls decided to stay in their present school. Ruby's parents decided she would attend alone.

"My parents only said, 'Ruby, you're going to go to a new school today, and you'd better behave.'"

Escorted to school by four US marshals sent by the president to protect her, Ruby and her mom walked to the school.

Ruby remembered, "There were barricades everywhere. There were cameras everywhere. I thought I'd stumbled into a parade. I actually thought it was Mardi Gras."

The marshals got Ruby safely inside the building, where she was taken to the principal's office. Ruby and her mom spent all day in the principal's office while white parents came to take their kids out of the school.

"Five hundred kids walked out of school that day, and I didn't know what was going on," remembered Ruby. "Because nobody explained anything to me. Finally the bell rang and someone came into the office and they said, 'School is dismissed. You can leave.' And I remember sitting there and thinking, 'Wow! College is easy.'"

The second day, Ruby and the marshals walked through larger, angrier crowds. People shouted threats. One person held up a child-sized casket with a black doll inside. But Ruby made it through the crowds and was shown to a classroom inside.

There were no kids in the classroom, but there was a teacher: Barbara Henry. Mrs. Henry was kind to Ruby, and they had fun learning together, but Ruby's teacher wasn't what she expected.

"I remember looking at her and thinking, 'She's white!' I'd never seen a white teacher before. She looked exactly like the people outside. She wasn't. I always say that she showed me her heart."

By December, school attendance at William Frantz Elementary had fallen to about twenty students. Ruby still wasn't allowed to see even that number. The principal had confined Ruby to her classroom. She couldn't play outside or eat in the cafeteria.

When winter gave way to spring, the protests stopped and the restrictions were lifted. Ruby was allowed to meet the other students. In the CBN interview, she remembered, "I was so excited. So I went in to play with them. This little boy looked at me and he said, 'I can't play with you. My mom said not to play with you because you're a n*gger.'[2]

"So that's what this is about?" Ruby realized. "It's not Mardi Gras and this isn't college. It's about me. It's about me and the way I look and the color of my skin. And in my mind, that was okay. Yes, he hurt my feelings, but I wasn't angry with him because I felt like he was explaining to me why he couldn't play with me."

Ruby understood that the boy was simply listening to his parents, in the same way she listened to her parents when they told her she'd be going to a new school. Attitudes and behaviors are often handed down in families.

---

2. The "n-word," as it is called, is an especially offensive word with a long history of white people using it to demean and insult Black people. Over time, Black people have used the word, but in a very different way. They have taken over the word as a way of reducing its power to offend and dehumanize. The n-word is now a term used only by Black people toward other Black people. It is not a word others should feel free to say even when they hear Black people saying it. By the way, not all Black people even say the n-word. When in doubt, don't say it!

Ruby didn't choose to take a stand by herself when she was six. It was her family's stand to change things for the better. And things did change, slowly. Returning to William Frantz Elementary the following year, Ruby had a new teacher and a room full of classmates, both white and Black.

When she grew up, Ruby launched a foundation and began sharing her story with students across the country. What started as her parents' decision to enroll Ruby in a new school became a cause Ruby grew into and stood for proudly.

In the fight against racism, Ruby holds a special place in history as the Black kindergartener who attended an all-white school alone. But Ruby was never really alone. She had her family's support and her faith in God to help her be strong.

Later in life, Ruby gave this biblical advice for others who stand up against racism: "Out of the commandments, the one you should keep is Love Thy Neighbor. That is the key. I have to care about you as a person and a human being. I really believe the longer I live that it really has everything to do with love."

Questions to Consider

- How would you feel if you were kept away from all your classmates like Ruby Bridges was?
- What would you say to the parents who pulled their kids out of William Frantz Elementary School when Ruby started attending?

CHAPTER 14

How to Do Reconciliation Right

Reconciliation is a big word that means healing a relationship that has been broken. The relationship can be between two people or it can be between two groups of people. All forms of reconciliation are, by their very nature, tied up with relationships.

When siblings fight over something, their relationship is damaged. If one child is jealous of another, their relationship suffers. When a relationship is damaged, it is best to be restored—or reconciled—in person, which is why parents often require siblings to apologize to each other face-to-face, then hug to show they've restored their relationship. Of course, sometimes kids do those things just because adults make them, but hopefully they mean it when they make up.

In Ruby Bridges' story, she could have ended up bitter toward all white people. That would have been very understandable. So many people did awful things just to keep Ruby and kids who looked like her out of a school that should have been open to everyone. Ruby would have had good reasons never to want to go to a school with another white person. No six-year-old should have to be a symbol of racial progress. But as Ruby got older and engaged in her journey of racial identity development, she chose reconciliation. No one can force this, and no one should try to make you reconcile until you're ready. But mending relationships is a key to racial justice.

The best example of reconciliation comes from the Bible. The Son of God becoming human in Jesus Christ—what theologians call the *incarnation*—demonstrates the truth that all reconciliation is relational. When God wanted to reconcile people to himself and to each other, God didn't send a tweet or a TikTok video; God sent his Son. Christ himself is the best guide for our reconciliation efforts. God took on a human body: "The Word became flesh and made his dwelling among us" (John 1:14). The Bible reveals that God is not some distant and mysterious force but a personal and loving Creator who wants an in-person relationship with the women, men, and children created in God's very image. But there's a problem.

Whenever we choose to rebel against God, we do not simply break a rule; we rupture a relationship. It's just like when our relationships with siblings or friends break down because we fight about something. When we disobey the Creator, we create spiritual distance between us and God. We become our own little gods by creating rules for ourselves and denying the true and living God. The story of human history is one of broken relationships between God and one another. Fortunately, God has a plan to reconcile all things.

Maybe you've heard this story—the gospel—lots of times before. Now it seems so familiar that you don't need to hear it again. But just like rewatching a movie you've seen before or rereading a book you've read once, if you go back and do it again, you might notice something new. Old truths can stand out in fresh ways when we hear them from new voices.

Even if someone isn't religious or doesn't follow a particular religion, they can still see that reconciliation is a matter of right and wrong. Reconciling people from diverse racial and ethnic boundaries opens channels of communication and understanding and moves communities toward welcoming each other in. The power of reconciliation holds true across times, places, and cultures. It rises above our natural tendencies to be self-centered in relationships and leads us to new heights of understanding others. Reconciliation is for everyone.

Let's talk about the "relationship" part of the ARC of Racial Justice. It considers the concept of reconciliation from a God-centered perspective. I believe one of the key tools in fighting racism is understanding the spiritual part of race relations.

Racial Justice Often Begins with Relationships

We sat on an assortment of couches, dining room chairs, and even coffee tables as we chitchatted politely but awkwardly following the murder of another unarmed Black person. I honestly, sadly, don't remember which specific incident because there are so many. But I do remember one particular story from that night.

A white husband and wife had befriended a Black husband and wife in my church. Each couple had children about the same age. Of course, their experiences had been very different because of race. One night when the Black and white couple were hanging out, the Black couple explained having "the talk" with their two Black teenage sons, explaining how they had to tell their sons how to survive being pulled over by the cops.

Turn on the dome light in the car if it's dark.

Don't make any sudden moves.

Keep your hands visible at all times.

Stay calm, no matter what the officer does.

All of this could mean the difference between an arrest, a beating, or even living or dying. The white husband told the group, "It never even crossed my mind to have that kind of talk with our white teenage sons." For both the white and the Black couple, it was a painful moment because it highlighted the different worlds their families lived in. At the same time, the white couple had learned more of the reality of what it is like to be Black in America. While the burden should never just be on Black people to "educate" white people—everyone needs to do their own work too—it was a moment of greater unity and deeper friendship. They moved farther along in the journey of racial reconciliation, and it happened through relationships.

As we have been learning, simply understanding the facts around racism will not change how things are done. Nor will being committed to changing things if you don't really understand or have a relationship with people who are different from you.

People need a personal motivation to shake up the regular patterns of racism in their own lives and in society. Often it is a relationship or friendship that changes a person's perspective. Reading a book about the Civil Rights movement can be helpful, but hearing the grief in the voice of someone who lived through it will leave a more lasting impression. Relationships make reconciliation real and motivate us to act.

How NOT to Do Reconciliation

Thankfully, I have only broken one bone in my life. When I was three or four years old, I fell off of a stool and broke my thumb. Of course, right after that my mom put a Band-Aid on my thumb and that fixed the broken bone . . . I hope you know that's not the right way to fix a broken bone. A Band-Aid wouldn't have healed my broken thumb. And I hope you know my mom is way too smart to try that! She took me to the doctor and now I barely even remember it happening.

But quick fixes for racial wounds are like putting Band-Aids on a broken arm. In order to properly fix the situation, to reconcile it to the way it should be, doctors are going to have to get involved. The bone may need to be rebroken so it can be set properly. It will probably need a cast. The hospital bills won't be cheap. And the arm will take time and physical therapy to heal and be useful again.

To do racial reconciliation in the way it should be done, everyone needs to realize that a one-time apology isn't going to fix the underlying problems in the system. Apologies are a great place to start, but fixing things means looking into the history of what went wrong and trying to set things right. This may mean that things will be painful all over again, just like when a doctor has to reset an arm break. It means making new rules and new systems to make up for the old ones that led to the inequalities we see in society today.

Are you ready to get started?

Questions to Consider

- What is one example of reconciliation from your own life?
- Why do you think relationships are important in reconciliation?
- Have you ever had "the talk" with your parents about interacting with police?
- How has God reconciled himself to you?
- If a one-time apology doesn't change the reason people fight, what would?

CHAPTER 15

Racial Justice in Action: Exploring Your Own Relationships to the Past

Uncovering the truth can be painful, whether you are digging into the ways you've been guilty of racism in the past or learning hard truths about a community you thought you knew. But pain is part of the process of healing. And healing requires you to do the painful work of confronting racism where you live.

Musical artists know a lot about pain and healing. In fact, there's a whole style of music dedicated to exploring the pain of life and how to understand it. It's called Blues music, and learning to deal with the blues of life can be a healthy way to channel your pain.

Learn About the Blues

The word *lament* isn't one you hear very often. As a noun, a lament is an expression of sadness you feel in your gut, in your bones. As a verb, it means to feel that sadness or to express it in a way that other people can hear. There's a book of the Bible—right between Jeremiah and Ezekiel—that's all about lament. In fact, it is called Lamentations. And if lament is important enough to have its own book in the Bible, it is important to incorporate into your life.

Most people don't like to dwell on sad things, but if you have not learned to lament, you have not learned to love. To love someone is to know and be known, which means opening oneself up to the possibility of being hurt by another. Think about the times someone's words or an argument has hurt you most. Was it with a stranger or with someone who you know really well, like a friend or a brother or sister? In love, we leave ourselves open to the failings and flaws of others. When love is betrayed and people hurt others in racist ways, it is cause for lament.

Those who have learned to lament will be able to sing their sadness. Blues music emerged in the Deep South, especially the Mississippi Delta, in the late-nineteenth century, and it is known for its use of certain chords and notes called "blue notes" to express a mood of sadness and feeling tired and worn. The music grew out of the souls of Black folks as they picked cotton in the Jim Crow era. They sang of broken hearts, love lost, and the unfairness of life. Even though the themes spoke of life's difficulties, singing the blues also helped lighten those difficulties. It expressed pain in the language of lyrics and melodies. The very act of singing or strumming that emotion helped strengthen the performers and the hearers for another day.

Every person and community dedicated to racial justice should have a playlist of songs devoted to lament. When we express lament through song, it has a way of lifting the soul out of despair. If we can put words to our hurt, then we can, in some sense, deal with the harm in our own way. Singing songs of lamentation turns our mourning into music and creates art out of anguish.

If you haven't had a chance to hear the blues, ask a parent or a librarian to help you find some to listen to. Most blues songs follow an AAB pattern. That means in each verse or stanza, the same line is repeated twice and the third line is a bit different. When you put them together, they tell a little story. Take for example the blues song, "Blues with a Feeling."

> **A**–Blues with a feelin',
> that's what I have today
> **A**–Blues with a feelin',
> that's what I have today
> **B**–I'm gonna find my baby,
> if it takes all night and day[1]

Maybe you can try to write your own blues song.

Look into Your School's Racial History

Remember how Pacific Bay Christian Academy was originally named Alma Heights in order to honor a KKK-supporting preacher? Segregation academies, as they were known, popped up all over the country in the years around the *Brown v. Board of Education of Topeka* ruling. They took the names of Confederate generals or racist leaders. They had mascots like Rebels or Colonels. Many schools started meeting in churches because they didn't have the funds to build a separate school building

---

1. Lyrics taken from "Blues with a Feeling," written and originally performed by Rabon Tarant, and included on the album *Slowly Goin' Crazy Blues* (Black & White, 1947).

before the government enforced desegregation in public schools. Of the thousands of segregation schools that were started in the 1960s and 70s, many are still around today, having celebrated their fiftieth anniversaries sometime recently.

Some schools, like Pacific Bay Christian Academy, have made great strides in correcting the wrongs committed by their founders. Others have simply added a paragraph to their student handbook saying they won't discriminate because of skin color, but they stop at doing more to add diversity to their student body. In any case, real change won't happen until the students and families who attend and support these schools give them reason to change.

It isn't only private schools that might have racist roots. In the years of the Great Migration, many white families moved out of the city into the surrounding countryside, swelling the populations of previously tiny towns. Schools in these small towns probably still don't have much diversity and may not see the benefits of a multiracial community if they suddenly happened to become one.

How can you discover your school's history on race? Start with the school's website. See if there is a section on the history of the school you can read. Ask your teachers what they know about the school's origin. Do you have any relatives who attended that school when they were kids? Ask them about it. And if all of those sources don't give you enough information, email your local newspaper to see if they can help you discover the school's origins and racial history. If you're in a private academy, a school that is connected to a church, or a school that started in the late 1960s or 1970s, you should pay careful attention to how and why your school got started. And remember, we usually like to tell the historical stories that make us or the people we like look good. Make sure you're getting the *full* story.

For these schools and the students like you who attend them, there must be an acknowledgment of the racism that initially launched their existence. To deal with the reality of racism in your school's history is to take a necessary step toward racial justice. This will require courage, because some people would rather ignore their past and pretend it didn't affect them. The truth is that historic racism affects individuals and communities in ways that may be hidden but are no less real. And only what is revealed can be healed.

A perfect record is not required for a school to make progress on issues of race, but honesty about where those issues came from is.

Questions to Consider

- Have you ever heard a blues song? Listen to one and try to write your own about racism.
- When was your school founded? And why?

Jameel's Fight

For white police officer Andrew Collins, February 8, 2006 was just another day to catch criminals selling drugs. For Jameel McGee, a Black man, it was the day he was arrested for a crime he did not commit. It was the day he was supposed to meet his newborn son for the first time. Instead, he found himself behind bars, accused of selling drugs.

Jameel, even though he was completely innocent and this was his first drug-related offense, was sentenced to ten years in prison, mostly because of the testimony of the arresting officer, Andrew Collins. Andrew wanted to be the top cop, not only in the overwhelmingly Black city of Benton Harbor, Michigan, where he worked, but in the state. To do so, he wanted to have as many convictions—when a person is determined to be guilty in a court of law—as possible, and Officer Collins was willing to lie on his paperwork to get them.

Let's fast forward a few years. Jameel is behind bars, angry about the injustice of the situation. Meanwhile, Officer Collins has progressed from lying on his paperwork to selling drugs himself. He was guilty of the same crime he falsely arrested Jameel McGee for back in 2006.

After serving three years in prison as an innocent man,

Jameel's conviction was thrown out and he was declared a free man. And as Jameel went free, Andrew headed to prison to serve an eighteen-month sentence.

Think about that for a minute. An innocent Black man was sentenced to ten years in prison for a drug-related offense (one he didn't even commit). A guilty white man was sentenced to eighteen months for the exact same offense (and he was actually guilty).

Throughout each man's time in prison, God was working. Jameel felt like God was asking him to let go of his anger and trust God to take care of things. For Andrew, God was encouraging him to accept responsibility for how he harmed others. To both men, God was expressing love for them.

In 2011, Jameel and Andrew met by chance at a church event called "Hoops, Hip-Hop, and Hotdogs" happening in Broadway Park in Benton Harbor. Andrew was there with the church that was putting on the event. Jameel was there with his now five-year-old son. Actually, that day at the park was the first time Jameel had spent any time with his son since his plans were interrupted by arrest five years earlier.

At the park, Jameel asked Andrew to explain to his son why his dad had missed so many years of his life. Andrew apologized, saying he was a messed-up person back then and he was sorry for the way he messed up Jameel's life. There was nothing he could do to give Jameel his time back, but he accepted responsibility for his actions. Jameel still wasn't happy about how things turned out, but he continued to trust God.

Fast forward again to 2015. Andrew was working with an organization that helps people who have been in prison find jobs. The director of the organization came to Andrew and said there was someone she'd like him to work with named Jameel McGee.

Time and again, God had brought these men together. And although Andrew had hurt Jameel deeply, robbing him of three years of his life because of his lies, they eventually developed a relationship. From working together to writing together to traveling around the country and telling their story, Jameel and Andrew have become friends.

If friendship can be possible between the corrupt white cop and the innocent Black man he sent to prison, it can be possible for anyone. But there has to be an easier way.

Questions to Consider

- When have you forgiven someone who has wronged you in the past?
- How have you sought forgiveness from someone you've wronged in the past?
- What does your relationship with that person look like today?

CHAPTER 16

How to Make Friends

Good news! No matter what your race happens to be, as a kid, you are a natural at something important, something adults really struggle with. What is it?

Well, Black pastor and author Thabiti Anyabwile explained it like this to a grown-up audience during a talk on "The Dos and Don'ts of Racial Reconciliation." With a smile on his face, Anyabwile jokingly teased the audience about how difficult it had become for most of them to make friends across racial and ethnic lines. He reminded them of how easy it used to be when they were kids. "Every one of us at three, or four, or five used to go up to people and say, 'Will you be my friend?' And what happened?" he asked the audience. "We got friends!"[1]

Ask almost anyone for suggestions about what to do about racism, and most people will say we need relationships with people who are different from us. Cross-cultural friendships are one of the most obvious ways to move farther down the road of racial justice. But making those friendships often feels harder than it should. As Anyabwile went on to tell his adult

---

1. Thabiti Anyabwile, "The Dos and Don'ts of Racial Harmony," speech, The Gospel Coalition 2015 National Conference, Orlando, FL, April 14, 2015.

audience, "At some point we stopped doing that because it became weird. I just think we should go back to being weird. And say, 'Hey, listen, I offer you friendship.'"

Fixing racism takes more than having one or two friends of color. Still, it's a great step in the right direction. And the good news is that making new friends is probably simpler than you think.

The Importance of Interracial Friendships

Studies have shown that kids with at least one close friendship with someone from a different race or ethnicity have better social skills. That means being able to listen better, to understand how other people are feeling, and to know how to act when you are with others.

How? Because friendships with people who have different backgrounds can give you a look into a different culture than your own. It lets you see that just because someone is different, it doesn't make them wrong. Why do some people like certain foods or hobbies? Why are some kids drawn to certain kinds of music or dance styles? If no one you know likes those types of food, hobbies, or music or dance styles, you may grow up thinking that liking those things is weird or wrong. If asked, maybe you'd say that everyone is allowed to be different, but inside you wouldn't feel like those differences are normal.

But remember that the image of God is incomplete if it leaves anyone out. Making friendships with people unlike yourself makes it easier to see the multiracial and multicultural makeup of God's image.

Having interracial friendships isn't just about learning to like others for who they are; it's important because it can help you accept yourself for who *you* are. Because we live in a country where white people, who have held the historical majority of the population, have decided what is "normal" or acceptable, any interest or behavior that falls outside this "normal" view can make someone think there's something wrong with them. When you have friends who don't fit society's view of "normal," trying to fit in with the expectations of white society becomes less important, so you can decide for yourself what things you like instead of feeling like you have to enjoy something just because society says so.

Unfortunately, studies have also shown that if you don't make interracial friendships when you are young, it's a lot harder to do when you get older.

Be a Humble Friend

The first step to having friendship, whether interracial or same-race, is humility not utility. That means remembering that every person has value simply because we are each an image of the Creator.

If your friendship is based on what the other person can give you or what you get out of your connection (maybe your friend has better video games or their dad makes the best cookies), your friendship is based on selfishness and it isn't friendship at all. Your motive for being friends with someone is important, so if you are only trying to be friends with a person of a different race or ethnicity for the benefits you'll get out of the relationship, it isn't really friendship.

The best relationships follow the example Jesus gave us. Philippians 2:3–8 (NIrV) says, "Don't do anything only to get ahead. Don't do it because you are proud. Instead, be humble.

Value others more than yourselves. None of you should look out just for your own good. Each of you should also look out for the good of others. As you deal with one another, you should think and act as Jesus did. In his very nature he was God. Jesus was equal with God. But Jesus didn't take advantage of that fact. Instead, he made himself nothing. He did this by taking on the nature of a servant. He was made just like human beings. He appeared as a man. He was humble and obeyed God completely. He did this even though it led to his death. Even worse, he died on a cross!"

Jesus offered his friendship to us, knowing the sacrifice it was going to cost him. If we want genuine friendships with others, it's going to cost us something too. The point of friendship isn't to be the same as our friends, but to see the image of God in them and to love them for who they are. It starts with humility—putting others ahead of ourselves—which can lead to unity, like we can have with Jesus because he was willing to sacrifice himself for us.

Friendship and Communication Basics

It's pretty safe to say that for you to be friends with someone, you have to do stuff together. Friends who don't have shared experiences or talk to each other are basically just strangers who know each other's names. But the possibility of being friends with someone from a different background actually does start before you hang out with them. Just like a house is built on a foundation, strong friendships are built on top of a few important ideas.

Kids who have interracial friendships start out by being comfortable around kids who don't look like them. You may think that the comfort comes after the friendship, but it actually happens before.

For the longest time I wouldn't even taste guacamole. If you've also never had it, it's a type of food, usually a dip for tortilla chips or a topping on various dishes, that's made up of smashed avocados and some other ingredients for flavor. It's green and shiny and I think I may have heard someone somewhere at some time say they didn't like it. So I wouldn't even try it . . . until I did. I was a full-grown adult and I finally decided to taste and see for myself. Now my kitchen seems bare if I don't have any avocados or guacamole in it. I love eating it and have found how it makes all kinds of different foods taste even better.

Sometimes we think about other people like I used to think about guacamole. We don't like how they look, or we heard someone once say something negative about them, so we don't even try to be friends. But the other thing that helps interracial friendships succeed is when kids, even before spending time together, have a positive attitude about other racial groups.

Many people make up their minds about other racial groups before they ever even meet. Maybe they've heard family members say bad statements about certain races or they've seen stereotypes of those races acted out in movies. However those bad opinions about other races are made, they make it almost impossible for interracial friendships to start off on the right foot. In order to make friendships well, you need to lay down the stereotypes and honestly believe that those who are different are valuable people who are made in God's image.

When you are comfortable around kids outside of your racial group and believe in their dignity, you'll be more likely to have a strong friendship. The next step is actually hanging out with them. Shared experiences build stronger relationships. They are the bricks that build on your foundation. These experiences can happen in the classroom through group projects or on the playground or outside of school hours.

If shared experiences are like bricks, conversations are like the mortar that helps bricks stick together. There are a few rules to having a good conversation with someone. If you can master these while you are young, you'll be well set up for a lifetime of good communication:

- **Listen well.** Actually listen when someone is talking and ask questions that relate to the topic. Don't use the time when the other person is talking to think up what you are going to say next.
- **Don't interrupt.** Interrupting someone might communicate that you don't care what they have to say, that what you are saying is more important. This can lead them to avoid talking to you in the future.
- **Be okay if a person does not want to talk.** Especially when the conversation is regarding race, be sensitive to the other person's comfort level. White people especially need to look for cues that people of color may not want to have another conversation about race. Your interest in issues of diversity is important, but if the other person does not seem to want to talk about it, that's okay. Respect their boundaries. Don't force a topic they don't want to discuss.
- **Make appropriate eye contact.** Turning your body and face toward someone tells them you are paying

attention to them. Don't stare at the smartphone or tablet when you're talking to someone.

- **Don't just ask questions.** Offer information about yourself too. The more you are willing to share, the deeper your relationship can be. Just make sure that you can trust the person you're sharing stuff with.
- **Don't be afraid to admit when you don't know something.** Especially if you are coming from a different background, there are probably a lot of things you won't know. It's always better to ask for understanding than to make assumptions or act like a know-it-all.
- **Look for common ground.** Find out what interests you share and talk about those things. When you feel like you have more in common with someone, the differences between you won't stop your friendship from moving forward.
- **Don't let arguments turn into cold silences.** Sometimes conversations will head toward arguments. This happens in every relationship, and it's just part of being human. Try not to panic or overreact in anger or anxiety. Remember the lessons about reconciliation. Reconciliation is especially important after arguments. Don't wait around for the other person to apologize. Let them know you value their friendship by taking the first step in making things right.

Race Is Felt

One way to have humility in cross-cultural relationships is realizing that this isn't just a matter of the head, it's a matter for the heart. Many people, particularly those in the racial majority, come at the issue of race like it is something to understand mentally. They think solutions come from good ideas and that people can fix things just by thinking about them more deeply. They don't realize that race is something other people feel in the bones.

Humble people recognize that racism has caused indescribable damage to whole communities of people. For members of the affected communities, talking about racism is more than a mental exercise. It's personal. It comes with smells, tastes, sounds, sights, and physical sensations. It carries with it injury, pride, and the commitment to carry on. Race is lived. Race is felt.

When a person of color shares something deeply personal, it would be wise for white people to listen and try to understand the experience before jumping in with advice on how they could fix things. Good friendships require both the head and the heart.

As you look for ways to include diversity in your friends, you have to know that meeting people from different racial and ethnic backgrounds will be harder for white people. Our society has been set up to keep white people segregated from people of color. It is possible for many white people to live their whole lives without any meaningful connections with racial and ethnic minorities. The intentional segregation of the races means many white people will have to go out of their way to meet people from different backgrounds.

The good news is you can develop the skills and commitment to break down those barriers, and find great friends in the process.

Questions to Consider

- How do you usually make friends?
- What do you like to do with your friends?
- Why do you think it is important to make friends with kids who don't look like you?
- What does "be a humble friend" mean to you?
- How can you listen well to someone else?
- Why would a white person feel race differently than a person of color?

CHAPTER 17

Racial Justice in Action: Building Relationships with Others

Building relationships with people is one of the most difficult things to do in life. Trying to build relationships with people from different backgrounds, who have different skills and speak with different vocabularies, makes it more difficult still. And yet, building relationships is also one of the most important things you can do as you fight racism. Keep reading to discover a few things that will help you become a better relationship-builder.

Do Your Homework First

Have you ever listened to your teacher explain a problem in class, then get tapped on the shoulder by a classmate who asks you how to solve the problem? The teacher just explained it to everyone! Weren't they listening? It can be annoying when it feels like people aren't willing to help themselves.

When people of color are asked basic questions about race

and how it affects them, it can feel like white people aren't willing to help themselves. There are all kinds of resources out there to help white people realize what Black people have been through, from bestselling books and news articles to magazine stories and movies. This book in your hands is just one of many that are available to help you know the basics of Black history.

Sometimes we treat people like the Alexa app from Amazon. You get the device and you connect it to the internet. Then when you have a question or want information, all you have to say is, "Hey, Alexa . . ." and ask your questions. People of color are not the human equivalent of an Alexa app. You shouldn't go to them with your questions without first doing some background research yourself. When you're constantly asking someone else to explain race and racism, you haven't done your homework.

This does not mean you can never ask anyone for help or engage in conversations about race. Please do! It does mean that you should not expect others to do the hard work of learning for you. Care about people enough to cover the basics on your own.

Be Real

It would be great to think that everyone wants to make friends for the right reasons, but some people are only interested in interracial friendships so they can show the world how not racist they are. Remember, trying to be friends with someone because of what you get out of it—and wanting to look like a good example of anti-racism in order to have people like you counts as getting something out of it—is just another form of selfishness.

For a friendship to be real, go into it with the right motives. Start on some common ground. Share an experience. Have a conversation. Don't try to collect interracial friendships like they are part of a game where you can level up your social status because of a diversity bonus.

If having a diverse group of friends is important to you for unselfish reasons, then start with the social circles you are already in. Maybe you already know someone in your school, church, or neighborhood, but you haven't put time or effort into the relationship before now. Start there and see where it goes. If you have nothing in common at all (which is pretty unlikely, since we all have some things in common), then maybe the friendship wasn't meant to be. Don't force something if it isn't going to be real. A good way to see if you have any common ground is to say, "Tell me about yourself," then listen.

Adding real friendships with people from other racial and ethnic backgrounds isn't just a goal for white people. Black people and people of color should make the effort to learn from one another too. Dialogues between racial and ethnic minorities are vital. Black people need to understand more of the Asian immigrant and Asian American experience. All of us need to hear from Native Americans. People of color have unique experiences, cultures, and histories. We are all dealing with the impact of white supremacy, and learning from other people who are dealing with racial and ethnic issues builds both awareness and alliances.

Start Where You Are

I came to faith because of an interracial friendship I had with a guy named Christopher, who everyone just called "Toph."

Toph and I didn't have a whole lot in common on the surface. We lived in the same town and we went to the same high school, but he was white and had an amazing jump shot and I was Black and could barely hit the basketball rim most times. However, Toph and I had freshman health class together first thing in the morning and we just started talking.

Soon we were lifting weights together at the YMCA and Toph started inviting me to his church's Wednesday night youth group, which was held in the gym of a different school than ours. So I started to go. The youth pastor at Toph's church would give these fifteen-minute mini-sermons and they were really good. I started to resonate.

Then my sophomore year, Toph invited me to come along to his youth group's winter retreat. I vividly remember it being winter because I can still smell the cabin with its wet socks and high school boy funk. But I also remember sitting down with Toph and the youth pastor and giving my life to Jesus. They asked me if I believed Jesus was God. I did (still do). They asked if I knew I was a sinner in need of salvation. I did (still am). They asked me if I'd like to accept Jesus' gift of salvation by believing he died in my place so I could be with him in heaven when I died. I did (praise God!). And we prayed a prayer and that was that. When I opened my eyes, I was a Christian. I didn't know everything that meant, but I knew it was real and I've been a Christian ever since.

My friendship with Toph wasn't because we were so alike. It was because he was a Christian who was genuinely curious about my life and was kind to me. He was interested in me as a person and concerned about my well-being. We clicked socially because he had a great sense of humor and he was fun to hang out with. We clicked spiritually because he loved God and he loved people.

Toph met me where I was and invited me into his youth group community. After spending time together, I felt like I had a place there, like I belonged there, even though I was different from everyone else in his youth group. That's what gave me hope that we don't all have to be the same to feel a sense of belonging.

How to Meet People of Different Racial and Ethnic Backgrounds

If growing your current relationships to better reflect the diversity of God's image isn't an option, you may have to expand your social network. I know, you're still young. It's not like you can hop in your car and drive to another city or buy yourself a plane ticket to go across the country. The truth is, there may be more diversity closer to home than you think. You just need to know where to look.

Ask your parents to plan a visit to a park in another part of town. Check out programs that might interest you at your local YMCA. See what libraries or bookstores in nearby communities have to offer. Join a city-wide sports program or club instead of just the ones at your own school. Go to a festival or parade celebrating people from a different racial and ethnic background. The American Indian Center in Chicago, for example, hosts an annual powwow that is open to the public.

Some of this will be trial and error. The point is to do something you already enjoy, but that opens the door to encountering people of other races and ethnicities.

Questions to Consider

- Who is one person you admire from a different race or ethnicity? Why do you admire them?
- Where might you make some new friendships with kids of other ethnicities?

Howard's Fight

When people hear about the nonviolent approach to challenging racism, they usually think of Martin Luther King Jr. But without the work and influence of a man named Howard Thurman, King may never have become the face of the Civil Rights movement in America.

It was Howard Thurman who many years earlier led a group of Black American leaders to Mohandas Gandhi—the man who helped lead a nonviolent independence movement in the nation of India—and who wrote about how nonviolence could be used by Black Christian leaders in the fight for civil rights. It was Howard Thurman who mentored leaders like James Farmer (who founded the Congress for Racial Equality) and Martin Luther King Jr. while he was getting his PhD at Boston University. Howard had a direct influence on the leaders of the Civil Rights movement, but one of his most important contributions took place not at a college but at a church. He was part of developing one of the first major interracial, interfaith communities in the United States.

Howard Thurman was born in Daytona Beach, Florida, on November 18, 1899. His father died when Howard was seven, and he was raised by his mom with help from her mother, a formerly enslaved Black person. At his grandmother's request, Howard often read the family's Bible aloud. His time spent in God's Word and his conversations with his grandmother about the rich spiritual life that made slavery bearable had a big impact on who Howard would become later in life.

When Howard was fourteen, he left his home in Daytona Beach to attend high school one hundred miles away in Jacksonville, Florida—one of only three Black high schools available in the state during the years of enforced segregation. Howard's family saved up enough money to send him to school by train, but buying the train ticket left him penniless. When Howard found out that his ticket didn't include his necessary luggage, he sat down and cried. Everything seemed to be lost before his life even got going, until a stranger—a Black man dressed in overalls—walked over and paid Howard's baggage fee. Because of the stranger's kindness (he never learned the man's name), Howard was able to continue his education.

After his studies in Jacksonville, Howard went on to Morehouse College, where it was rumored that he read every book in the college's library. Around this time, Howard was a popular speaker to mixed-race audiences at student and youth events organized by the YMCA. His experiences speaking to interracial groups and his strong faith in God gave him a new vision for the American church.

Howard Thurman moved from speaker to pastor to professor of religion, always encouraging others to be rooted in their faith, guided by the Holy Spirit, and to live at peace with all. Then in 1944, Howard got the opportunity to put his advice into practice by co-founding the Church for the Fellowship of All Peoples in San Francisco, California.

The church was specifically designed to be multicultural,

a place where people of all races, ethnicities, and faith backgrounds could worship together in peace. At a time when segregation was still the law of the land, Howard Thurman (who was Black) and co-founder Alfred Fisk (who was white) tried to create a space where all people were welcomed and recognized to be made in the image of God.

Howard Thurman once said that the Spirit of God moving in the hearts of people often calls them to act against the spirit of their times. Although today, welcoming all people may seem like a common sense idea for a church, at the time churches like Fellowship were almost unheard of. It was revolutionary.

No one can fight racism alone. We need a community of people to help us on the way. If you don't belong to a community where your ideas can be heard and your worth as one of God's image bearers is recognized, it is time to find one . . . or time to start one like Howard Thurman did.

The ARC of Racial Justice requires us to make relationships with people of different racial and ethnic backgrounds. This can be difficult, but the road toward racial reconciliation would be impossible to walk down by yourself.

Questions to Consider

- Howard Thurman experienced the kindness of a stranger at the train station on his way to school. How has someone shown you kindness like that?
- How is your church like the Church for the Fellowship of All Peoples?

CHAPTER 18

How to Build Diverse Communities

Maybe you hear the word *community* and think about the neighborhood where you live. Your neighborhood is one kind of community, but there are lots of other communities you probably belong to. A community is a group of people who share something in common.

With your neighborhood, you share the street you live on or the building you live in. This kind of community is naturally made up of people who happen to be nearby. The kids in your classroom are another example of this kind of community. This might also include the kids you sit with at lunch or hang out with on the playground.

Some communities are organized around a common interest. Sports teams are communities. Book clubs are communities. Video games can be communities too. These communities provide people with some built-in things to talk about, to get excited over, and to participate in together. For Christians, the built-in community is the church, organized around Jesus Christ.

Every community, from cabins at summer camp to your homeroom class in school, can provide its members with a sense of belonging through shared experiences, common phrases, and inside jokes. But communities who actively try to keep certain people out because of their race or culture are twisting them into something bad.

So what can we do to make sure the communities we belong to are good for everyone?

Diversity, Equity, and Inclusion

When I was in junior high and high school, I loved school dances. Even though I was bad at basketball, I could dance really well. Every time me and my best friend, Malcolm, got on the dance floor, people would clear a space and make a circle around us to watch our moves. I knew that I just had to wait for the right song to come on and I could turn the party up. But I know for a lot of people, dances are filled with anxiety. Will you go or won't you? Will they play the music you like? Will anyone ask you to dance?

Building racially diverse communities can be like school dances in some ways. Diversity, equity, and inclusion are all different and are all needed for a community to really reflect God's diverse image. Robert Sellers, chief diversity officer at the University of Michigan, compares diversity, equity, and inclusion (DEI) to a dance. He says, "Diversity is where everyone is invited to the party. Equity means that everyone gets to contribute to the playlist. Inclusion means that everyone has the opportunity to dance."[1]

It's important to realize that just because a community has racial variety, it isn't necessarily working toward racial justice.

---

1. Defining DEI," University of Michigan, https://diversity.umich.edu/about/defining-dei/.

Diversity is a great goal, but it is only part of the picture. Too many people of color have been invited to join communities of mostly white people only to find that they are valued for their presence but not for the way they see things.

Diversity by itself is little more than pretending to pursue racial justice. Equity has to come alongside the diversity efforts in order for the variety of voices to be heard as equal. If diversity and equity are happening, but there's no inclusion, then it doesn't really matter if everyone is invited to the party and everyone is equally important. If they aren't included in the decisions that affect them, they might as well be silent.

A truly healthy community means that different people get invited to the party, they get to help pick the music, and others invite them to dance and have fun. Sports teams, church groups, book clubs, lunch tables, playground friends, or whatever kind of community you create—all of them must include diversity, equity, and inclusion to successfully mix racial justice into the makeup of the community.

Make a Plan, Work the Plan

I got my license as soon as I turned sixteen. My first car was a gray 1984 Buick Regal—it was basically a tank on wheels. It burned oil, and I would sink down in the seat at stoplights because I was so embarrassed about the white smoke billowing from the hood at all times. But I loved that car. I kept the gas tank full and even learned how to install a subwoofer so I would not just hear my music, I would *feel* the bass.

That old, huge, partially broken car represented freedom. As soon as I got it, I started listing all the places I wanted to go on my own or with friends—the movies, the mall, the beach.

If it was possible to drive there, and my old car could make it, I was going. But I always had a destination in mind, and I made sure I knew how to get there. I even had a printed map in the back seat in case I got turned around (this was before smartphones, when you couldn't just type in your destination).

Just like you need a map to find your way when driving, you need a map to make sure you're on the right course on the journey toward racial justice. It also has to be a map that will clearly get you to your destination. The bridge between a desire and a destination is a plan.

To make a plan for a racially inclusive community, structure it around the ARC of Racial Justice—have sections for awareness, relationships, and commitment. In each of those sections list at least three actions you and your community will take. But don't just leave it at that. Write down more details. For instance, if you make a plan to build awareness by watching documentaries about the history of race, also write down when and how. For example, you could make plan to "Watch one documentary film about racial history every three months." Or in the relationships section you could say, "Go to a festival, play, or community event and interact with people from a different culture at least two times per year." Make your goals as specific as possible, and you will have a better chance at success. Finally, share the plan. Scientific studies show that when people share their plans they are much likelier to stick to the plan and achieve their goals.

Making a plan to set up a diverse community where everyone has a voice and people are included in real ways is hard. Haaaarrrrrd. But after the hard work gets done, the result is a community that more fully reflects the image of God. The outcome is worth the effort.

Questions to Consider

- What is the most diverse community you are already part of?
- What communities do you belong to?
- How would you define diversity, equity, and inclusion in your own words?
- How could you encourage greater diversity in one of your existing communities?

CHAPTER 19

Racial Justice in Action: Sharing Your Passion

Like Scottie Pippen and Michael Jordan on the Chicago Bulls, intention and commitment make a great team. An intentional commitment to fighting racism can be as awe-inspiring to watch as it is to observe a dynamic duo in action on the court. It takes time and dedication, but eventually could become an inspiration to others as they watch you work. Commit to fighting racism by picking a few of the methods below and get started!

Start a Book Club

Books are windows into the lives of others. Books are also mirrors, allowing us to see reflections of ourselves in a story's characters. Emily Style explained this. She is the founding co-director of the National SEED Project, an organization that partners with schools, organizations, and communities to "develop leaders who guide their peers in conversational communities to drive personal, organizational, and societal change toward social justice."[1]

One of the best ways to develop your awareness of racism in society is to immerse yourself in books written by those who have experienced it firsthand. Books that have received the Coretta Scott King Book Award are a great place to start. The award commemorates the life and work of Dr. Martin Luther King Jr. and honors his wife, Mrs. Coretta Scott King, for her courage and determination to continue the work for peace and world brotherhood.

And books are doors that help us connect with other people. I've never met you, but I know that you read books. I know that you are interested in fighting for racial justice in a broken world. Based just on those things, I think we'd get along. In fact, readers and authors exist in a very interesting kind of community, separated by distance and time, but united by the fact that we're part of the same conversation about the book's subject—in this case, race. And as our community is off to such a good start already, I think it's time to open it up and create your own book club, where you can have conversations with other people about the things you read.

The idea behind starting a book club is pretty simple.

- Gather some kids who you know are readers.
- Agree together on which book to read.
- Read the book during an agreed-upon timeframe (many book clubs read one book per month).
- Get together at the end of the timeframe, or maybe

1. "Enacting What We Believe," The National SEED Project homepage, https://www.nationalseedproject.org/.

check in once per week (you could share some snacks too).

- Discuss the book. What stood out to you? What did you like? What didn't you like? What did you need help to understand better?
- Agree on the next book to read.
- Ask your teachers if you can do a book study group and get credit or extra credit for class. You should do a book club about race no matter what, but why not boost your GPA in the process?

When you think about the kinds of books you want to read, consider what you want to get out of the reading experience. If you want your club to be organized around racial justice, read books that would help you understand where other people are coming from. Both fiction and nonfiction books can help you. Feel free to start with a book you've already read and enjoyed. You could even start with this book!

Second, use your book club invites to put together as diverse a group as possible. Every group, especially those focused on learning about race and ethnicity, benefits from hearing different people speak about how they see the world. Although it may feel uncomfortable, it is alright to intentionally seek racial diversity in a group.

As you begin your book discussions, start with a story from your own life. In some groups, members may not know each other very well, and personal stories can help build trust and show that it's okay for everyone to share.

You may even want to start with a few questions about the book club community itself. What are their hopes for the group? Why did they decide to join you? How did they get interested in the topic of racial justice? Letting other people share their stories helps them feel seen and builds trust so you can talk about the hard stuff that might be found in the books.

For a list of specific book recommendations, check out "Some Books to Read About Race" in the appendix of this book.

Help Others Understand Why Diversity Is Awesome

Although most people say that diversity is a good thing, many don't follow through in their actions. It could be because they don't understand *why* diversity is awesome.

It's an easy mistake to think that when something is important to you, the rest of the world will agree it's important. Really, you shouldn't assume that everyone thinks the same way on racial justice or that they know all the things you've learned. Some people think racial justice is just about Black people talking about their feelings or complaining when things don't go their way. They could hardly be more wrong. In reality, these racial justice resisters are afraid that they might lose their place in society or that they might have to feel what it is like when things stop going their way. When people take the time to understand what racial justice really is and why it is important, they may see the reason to change society for the better. For example, a lot of studies have shown that having diversity on a team helps that team make better decisions, because members can bring all kinds of different ways of looking at an issue.

The best thing to do is to talk to people one-on-one and see why they think the way they do. Invite them to read a book you enjoyed that talked about racial justice and ask them for a book recommendation of their own. People are much more open to trading information when they feel they are not in a one-sided conversation, with you trying to convince them you are right. If you try talking to a big group of people about racial justice, some may either ignore you or feel like they are part of a majority who disagree about the importance of racial justice (even though people who think racial justice isn't important are actually the minority).

Write a Personal Statement on Racial Justice

Putting racial justice into practice in your community starts with a clear understanding of what racial justice means to you. Lots of businesses and organizations have official written statements about racial justice, but this one is just for you. Having your own definition and action plan spelled out on paper is good practice so you can have something to refer to when people ask you questions.

You could start with writing down your thoughts on diversity, equity, and inclusion. Or you might make an audio or video recording of yourself talking about what you believe about racial justice and how you will pursue it. Another idea is to use some form of art to communicate your ideas about racial justice. Maybe you write a poem, paint a picture, shape a sculpture, or compose a song. Express yourself in a way that is true to your creativity and use that to talk about an important topic such as racial justice.

Sharing your personal statement with other people in your community helps them see that you've put time and thought into issues related to race. It also provides your community with a way to hold you accountable for putting these thoughts into action. Just having a statement isn't the same as putting that statement to use. Actions must back up the words on the page (or whatever you create).

Even if you never show anyone else your statement, it is worthwhile to go through the process of creating it. Having conversations with others on racial justice, reading books from people who are different from you, and developing interracial friendships will all be necessary to writing a good statement.

Questions to Consider

- If you were going to start a new community, what ideas and values would it be based on? How would you build diversity into it from the start?
- What are some of the benefits of a diverse community?
- What things would you include in your personal statement on racial justice?

PART 3:
COMMITMENT

Rosa's Fight

B uses played an important role in Rosa Parks' life. Born on February 4, 1913, she was raised by her mother, Leona McCauley, and her grandparents, Rose and Sylvester Edwards, on their farm in Pine Level, Alabama. Rosa grew up when segregation ruled the South. She attended school in a run-down one-room schoolhouse with the other Black children. She and her fellow first- through sixth-grade students had to walk to school, while the white students in Pine Level rode school buses to their own (new) school building.

Rosa was a good student who was hoping to become a teacher like her mother. In high school, she took special classes from the Alabama State Teachers College, but when her grandmother got sick, followed by her mother, Rosa had to drop out of school to care for her family. She was no quitter though. After finding work and getting married, Rosa Parks returned to school with her husband's encouragement and finished her high school education.

Rosa had a passion for racial justice from an early age. Members of the Ku Klux Klan often drove by the farm where she grew up, but her grandparents stood their ground against intimidation. Her dedication to fighting against injustice was one of the things she and her husband, Raymond Parks, bonded over.

After she and Raymond married, Rosa worked as a seamstress for a T-shirt factory in Montgomery, Alabama. Raymond was a barber who also worked with the National Association for the Advancement of Colored People (NAACP). It was dangerous to be a member of the NAACP and to fight for the rights that were regularly denied to Black people. Organization members were often singled out and attacked to stop them from trying to change the racism built into the Southern lifestyle. But like her grandparents who faced down the Ku Klux Klan, Rosa boldly joined the NAACP in December 1943 to work with her husband for change. Rosa became the Montgomery chapter's youth leader as well as secretary to NAACP president E.D. Nixon.

Rosa still worked as a seamstress during the day, but at night she fought for justice in the cases of discrimination, violence, and murder that came across her desk through her NAACP work. Then in 1955, she became a case herself.

On December 1, 1955, Rosa Parks was arrested for refusing to give up her bus seat so a white man could sit down. Buses in Montgomery (and across the South) were strictly segregated with whites-only seats in the front and seats for Black people in the back. Black passengers were also made to step on at the front of the bus to pay the driver, then step off the bus and walk to the rear entrance so they wouldn't walk past the white riders.

As Rosa rode home from a long day of work, a large group of white people boarded the bus. When the driver noticed a few of them were standing, he stopped the bus and moved the official line that separated the white and Black seating areas. When she sat down, Rosa was in the Black section, but now she was sitting in the white section and a white man couldn't sit down while she refused to move.

The way the laws in Birmingham had been written, bus drivers actually had the "powers of a police officer of the city while in actual charge of any bus for the purposes of carrying out the provisions" according to the segregation code. When Rosa didn't move, the real police came and arrested her.

Some people have said that Rosa didn't move for the white man because she was physically tired from working a long day as a seamstress, but Rosa disagreed with that statement.

"People always say that I didn't give up my seat because I was tired, but that isn't true," she wrote in her autobiography, *Rosa Parks: My Story.* "I was not tired physically, or no more tired than I usually was at the end of a working day. I was not old, although some people have an image of me as being old then. I was forty-two. No, the only tired I was, was tired of giving in."[1]

After she was bailed out of prison, she and NAACP president E.D. Nixon worked to set things right with regard to bus segregation. At first, they planned a twenty-four-hour bus boycott for the day of Rosa's court trial. Black people were advised not to ride Montgomery's buses on December 5, 1955. But then they decided to go further and push for lasting change. Black women organized car pools, printed flyers, and walked to and from work. With help from a passionate young minister named Dr. Martin Luther King Jr., what started as a twenty-four-hour boycott lasted 381 days. Together, they brought the city to a standstill and forced white city and business leaders to change their policies.

Rosa's case made it all the way to the US Supreme Court, which ruled that bus segregation was unconstitutional, and

---

1. Rosa Parks, *Rosa Parks: My Story* (New York: Puffin Books reprint edition, 1999), 116.

the boycott ended when the court's written order arrived in Montgomery.

Although her case brought a victorious ruling against seg-regation, Rosa was one of many who suffered during and after the boycott. She was fired from her job as a seamstress and no one would hire her. She was shunned by Black people who disagreed with her progressive stance against Jim Crow laws—those who thought the best way was to not make trouble.

Eventually she moved to Detroit, Michigan, where she found work in Congressman John Conyers' office, supporting his efforts for national civil rights.

Then in 1987, at the age of seventy-four, Rosa co-founded the Rosa and Raymond Parks Institute for Self Development with her longtime friend Elaine Eason Steele. Through the institute, Rosa traveled the country on a bus, speaking about her experiences and continuing to fight for racial justice. The institute also set up the Pathways to Freedom program, which allows students to travel to significant places along the Underground Railroad and the Civil Rights movement, learning history lessons in a hands-on way.

The girl who wasn't allowed to ride a bus to school became the woman arrested for refusing to give up her bus seat, and she eventually became the woman sending out busloads of kids to learn about racial justice.

Questions to Consider

- What is one thing that surprised you about Rosa Parks' story?
- What could you do to emulate the courage and commitment of Rosa Parks?

CHAPTER 20

How to Work for Racial Justice

Just a few weeks before the end of the Montgomery Bus Boycott, Martin Luther King Jr. gave a speech at the opening of the Montgomery Improvement Association (MIA) Institute on Nonviolence and Social Change. He said, "It is true that as we struggle for freedom in America we will have to boycott at times. But we must remember as we boycott that a boycott is not an end within itself." Rather, he explained, "The end is reconciliation; the end is redemption; the end is the creation of the beloved community."

To some, the "beloved community" sounds like a place where everyone is happy and nothing bad ever happens, but Dr. King wasn't talking about some made-up world. Really, he was talking about a community that is formed and fueled. And when a community is fueled by love, it moves forward in positive ways.

In his roadmap to racial justice, *Where Do We Go from Here*, Dr. King wrote, "Power at its best is love implementing the demands of justice. Justice at its best is love correcting everything that stands against love."[1] Love is not a mere feeling of affection. In the beloved community, love is an action that uses power to bring about justice.

For example, if your friend is about to walk into a busy street with cars whizzing by, but they have no idea because they are looking down at their phone, what would you do? Would you just keep watching and hope they look up? I hope not! I hope you would run, shout, wave your arms, even push them out of the way if it kept them from getting hit by a car.

> "Power at its best is love implementing the demands of justice. Justice at its best is love correcting everything that stands against love."
>
> **Dr. Martin Luther King Jr.**

What would you do if you saw a person walking into a busy street, but it was not your friend? What if the person was a stranger? Should you react any differently? Shouldn't you still do everything you can to prevent that person from getting hurt even if you do not know the person? Unfortunately, many white Christians are satisfied with the way things are, so they have no desire to change. They might be willing to rush to help someone very close to them, but when it is someone they do not know very well, they are too afraid or too uncaring to get involved. They can come up with all kinds of reasons for not taking action: The person is too far away. I don't know them—what if they are mean? What if I end up scaring them with my shouting and waving? What if I get hurt in the process?

---

1. Martin Luther King Jr., *Where Do We Go from Here: Chaos or Community?* (Boston: Beacon, 1968), 37–38.

People come up with all sorts of "reasons" to stay out of a situation when they don't really want to be involved. But the simplest question is, "What does it look like to love my neighbor in this situation?" If we love our neighbor, we'll risk what it takes to prevent harm and make things right. And people of color have been—and are still being—harmed by racism. History has shown us how people of color have not simply wandered into a busy street; racism pushed them into the road and forced them into life-threatening situations.

If Christians really want to love their neighbor, they will look deeply at the ways society has endangered people of color. They'll start taking apart the unjust systems that favor white people over all others. It is one matter to recognize that all people are made equal and have built-in value. It is another to try to fix the ways the image of God has been made less by the systems and rules in our society.

The beloved community that Martin Luther King Jr. talked about is possible, but it will take more than having good feelings about people who are different from us. It means putting our love into action, committing to help others by setting the broken system right.

Love for God and Neighbor

Throughout Jesus' public ministry, the religious leaders tried to make him look foolish by asking him difficult questions. After correctly answering a series of such questions, one of the leaders was impressed, so he asked Jesus a question that the smartest people had been debating for years: "Of all the commandments, which is the most important?" (Mark 12:28).

Jesus summed up the most important commands of the

Christian faith like this: "'Love the Lord your God with all your heart and with all your soul and with all your mind and with all your strength.' The second is this: 'Love your neighbor as yourself.' There is no commandment greater than these" (Mark 12:30–31). Jesus said the core of Christianity is love for God and love for neighbors. This love is where the call for racial justice comes from.

Did you see how Jesus tied the love of God to the love of our neighbors? The greatest command is to love God with your entire being: heart, soul, mind, and strength. We don't leave anything back when we give ourselves to God. But how do we (and others) know that we love God with our whole selves? Love of God is shown through our love for others.

It's impossible to love God and hate those created in God's own image.

It's impossible to love God and hate those created in God's own image. Jesus' disciple John put it this way: "Anyone who loves God must also love their brother and sister" (1 John 4:21). Or as Fannie Lou Hamer (an awesome champion of racial justice we'll learn about later) put it, "Ain't no such thing as I can hate anyone and hope to see the face of God."[2]

The apostle Paul builds on the necessity of love in 1 Corinthians 13:1–3:

> If I speak in the tongues of men or of angels, but do not have love, I am only a resounding gong or a clanging cymbal. If I have the gift of prophecy and can fathom

2. Alice Walker, "Can't Hate Anybody and See God's Face," *New York Times*, April 29, 1973, https://timesmachine.nytimes.com/timesmachine/1973/04/29/97135122.pdf?pdf_redirect=true&ip=0.

all mysteries and all knowledge, and if I have a faith that can move mountains, but do not have love, I am nothing. If I give all I possess to the poor and give over my body to hardship that I may boast, but do not have love, I gain nothing.

The reason Christians should be involved in the racial justice movement comes from a responsibility to love. No amount of fancy words, deep knowledge, or personal sacrifice will amount to anything if they do not communicate love to our brothers and sisters. You cannot fight against racism without love.

Bearing Witness to Christ

Jesus called his followers to bear witness about him throughout the world (Acts 1:8). To bear witness means to tell the truth about the things you've seen and experienced.

These days, bearing witness has taken the form of "smartphone journalism." According to the Pew Research Center, 85 percent of Americans own smartphones.[3] This means the vast majority of people have cameras and microphones to record events as they happen or livestream them to social media sites like Facebook, Twitter, and TikTok. These videos of real-life events are then seen by millions of people, helping them see events for themselves so they can bear witness to the truth.

Smartphone journalism has made us aware of police brutality, helped prove people innocent of crimes, and exposed other injustices that would have otherwise been hidden or

---

3. https://www.pewresearch.org/internet/fact-sheet/mobile/.

covered up. Bearing witness is an important way to help others understand what Black people are going through, but it is also a biblical concept that calls Christians to help the world understand what Jesus went through for us.

In Matthew 25, Jesus so closely identifies with those who experience hard times that he says to serve them is to serve *him*. When we feed the hungry, clothe the naked, look after the sick, and visit people in prison, we have done the same to Christ himself. He says, "Truly I tell you, whatever you did for one of the least of these brothers and sisters of mine, you did for me" (Matt. 25:40). To care for those who experience injustice, including racism, is to bear witness to Christ himself and to declare his goodness through our words and actions.

Questions to Consider

- Why are both love and power necessary to create the beloved community?
- Why might someone *not* want to be in a beloved community?
- What does Jesus say is the greatest commandment?
- What does loving your neighbor have to do with racial justice?
- Can you think of a time when you or someone you know bore witness to racial justice and loving their neighbor?

CHAPTER 21

Racial Justice in Action: Making a Difference in Your Community

Fighting racism isn't just about changing your mind—it's about changing your actions too. At the end of reading this book, you've got to go out and work the plan. That's the only way to make a difference in your community. Others will see your work and, hopefully, join in. Below are a few ways you can get your whole community involved in the fight!

Budget for Justice

Most kids don't have paying jobs, so you may think there's not much you can do money-wise in the fight for racial justice. Think again. Kids have been engaged in philanthropy (raising money for charities to help people in need) for a long time.

At the age of nine, Jahkil Jackson founded Project I Am to help homeless people in Chicago through Blessing Bags filled with body care items, a towel, socks, and some snacks. According to a feature in the *Chicago Tribune*, Jahkil has been passionate about helping the homeless ever since his great-aunt brought him along to hand out chili and soup to a homeless tent community when he was five.[1] With the help of his parents, friends, and elementary school, Jahkil gathered supplies and started distributing Blessing Bags. His efforts were recognized in 2017 with a Barron Prize for Young Heroes, then tweeted about by former president Barack Obama. As of December 2020, Project I Am has provided over thirty-five thousand blessings throughout the world.

Other kids have started charities to fight cancer (check out Grace Callwood's We Cancerve Movement), to combat climate change (look up Isha Clarke's Youth Vs. Apocalypse), and to provide books and other resources to underserved communities (search for Aniyah Ayres' Aniyah's Mission). Some have started fundraisers to provide for existing charities, like Adom Appiah did through Ball4Good, an organization that has raised more than $70,000 for sixteen different charities in his area.

If you want to start raising money for the cause of racial justice, here are a few ideas to get you started:

- Make and sell your own original artwork
- Instead of asking for presents for your birthday or holidays, ask people to donate money to an organization you pick
- Collect books, clothes, and backpacks to be given to schools in underserved communities
- Set up a donation bin for school supplies at your church or school

---

1. Heidi Stevens, "10-Year-Old's 'Blessing Bags' Mission Earns Him National Acclaim," *The Chicago Tribune,* posted September 27, 2017, https://www.chicagotribune.com/columns/heidi-stevens/ct-life-stevens-wednesday-10-year-old-helps-homeless-0927-story.html.

- Plant a garden and either donate the fruits and veggies, or sell them and donate the profits
- Host a walk-a-thon, swim-a-thon, bike-a-thon, dance-a-thon, anything-a-thon and ask people to sponsor you as you do your thing for a specific length of time

The important thing isn't the amount of money you raise but the heart you have while you give. And giving back is definitely part of God's vision for his people. Here's how Jesus talked about giving in Mark 12:41–44:

Jesus sat down opposite the place where the offerings were put and watched the crowd putting their money into the temple treasury. Many rich people threw in large amounts. But a poor widow came and put in two very small copper coins, worth only a few cents. Calling his disciples to him, Jesus said, "Truly I tell you, this poor widow has put more into the treasury than all the others. They all gave out of their wealth; but she, out of her poverty, put in everything—all she had to live on."

Whether you have a lot or a little, whether you can raise millions of dollars or just a few coins, it is important to give to those in need because doing so is giving back to God.

Ask Your School or Church to Host a Freedom School

Back in 1964, the Council of Federated Organizations (COFO) coordinated the Mississippi Freedom Summer Project, otherwise known as Freedom Summer. This project brought hundreds of volunteers to Mississippi to help register Black voters and to educate kids whose local schools weren't equipped with the same resources as those in wealthier neighborhoods.

Freedom schools taught basic academic skills like reading and provided meals to kids. They took place in the summer when parents might have struggled to both work and watch their kids. By helping kids not lose what they learned throughout the school year, these Freedom schools helped kids start strong in the fall. Not only that, they helped parents get involved in their communities and get equipped to make real changes through voting power.

More than fifty years later, Freedom schools are still around. The Children's Defense Fund (CDF) has built on the original Freedom school model and adapted it for modern times. Schools or churches can become host sites for these modern Freedom schools to provide kids with six weeks of education and opportunities to get involved in their communities. Although it will cost the kids nothing to attend these schools, the host sites need to raise money to make sure the participants have food to eat, books to read, and basic educational resources.

Churches that have Vacation Bible School programs should already be familiar with some of the needs a Freedom school will have. In any case, it is worthwhile to look up the CDF Freedom School program and ask an adult whether it would be possible for your school or church to host one.

Run for Student Government

In seventh grade, our principal gave students permission to start our very first student government. We were all excited because that meant elections for officers like president, vice president, secretary, and treasurer.

I ran for president and I won! Actually two of us won. The principal said we had to have co-presidents, so another class-mate and I shared the role. I really appreciated the experience because I had to write a campaign speech, think of all the ways I wanted to make the school better, listen to my classmates (including some I normally did not speak to), and learn to talk to adults about serious topics.

Running for, and possibly serving, in office is a hands-on way for you to learn what it's like to make the rules and to make them with different kinds of people in mind. Who knows? Maybe one day it's president of student government and the next it's president of the United States!

Questions to Consider

- How might you raise money for an organization that fights racism? How could you get your friends involved in your efforts?
- What would you want to learn in a Freedom school?
- If you were elected to student government, what would you do to make things fairer between people of different races and ethnicities?

Tamir's Fight

A borrowed toy gun, a concerned citizen who called 9-1-1, a rookie police officer who lied on his job application, and two seconds of time. These were a few of the factors that led to the murder of twelve-year-old Tamir Rice in 2014.

On November 22, a Saturday, the weather in Cleveland, Ohio, was the warmest it had been in over a week. Tamir Rice took the opportunity to play outside of the Cudell Recreation Center, about a block from his home. Like boys his age, Tamir enjoyed playing with toy guns—not that his mother approved—but the one he borrowed from a friend on that fateful day was broken. The orange tip on the Airsoft gun (a toy gun that shoots plastic pellets and is made to look like a real gun), which identified it as a toy, had broken off.

As he played, a concerned citizen called 9-1-1. The caller said there was a man—"Probably a juvenile"—pointing a gun—"Probably fake"—at people on the playground. The dispatcher sent police to investigate, but they forgot to mention that it was probably a child playing with a toy.

Videos show the police car driving across the grass to the gazebo where Tamir was playing. Within two seconds of their arrival, before the police car even came to a full stop, Officer

Timothy Loehmann was out of the car and had shot Tamir twice from a distance of less than ten feet. Even if the officer had shouted a warning (which not all eyewitnesses said happened), less than two seconds is not enough time for a person to respond.

Then the police officers just stood there until a police detective and an agent from the FBI showed up to treat Tamir's injuries. When Tamir's fourteen-year-old sister tried to see what happened to her brother, police tackled her, put her in handcuffs, and placed her in the back of a police car.

A few minutes later, Tamir's mother arrived, having been told by a couple of neighborhood boys that her son had been shot by the police. And when Tamir's mom got to the site of the shooting, police officers threatened to arrest her if she wasn't going to calm down. She was given the option of either going with Tamir to the hospital or being forced into the police car next to her fourteen-year-old daughter.

Tamir died the next day. He is remembered by loved ones for being athletic and artistic, for being a caring son, and for loving a good joke.

In the months following Tamir's death, the Justice Department looked at the evidence to decide whether the officers involved—Timothy Loehmann, who fired the shot, and Frank Garmback, who drove the police car—were criminally responsible for what happened. A prosecutor was assigned to speak on behalf of Tamir, but he did little to hold the police officers accountable.

It was decided that Timothy Loehmann was justified in shooting Tamir because he thought the boy was reaching for a real weapon. Eventually, the case against the officers was dismissed. Neither was punished for his role in killing a child.

The system failed Tamir Rice. It wasn't just that someone called 9-1-1 to report him for playing with a gun (though that may not have happened if Tamir had been white). It wasn't just that police officers made assumptions about Tamir based on his skin color and started shooting before their car had even stopped. It wasn't just that the court system failed to hold anyone responsible for Tamir's death. It was all of those things together. And more.

Officer Timothy Loehmann shouldn't have even been on duty that day because he had lied about his work history on his job application—which got him fired a few years after shooting Tamir. Loehmann had previously been a police officer in Independence, about thirteen miles south of Cleveland, but he resigned when the police chief there said he showed "a pattern of a lack of maturity" that time and training wouldn't be able to fix.[1] Loehmann was then hired by the city of Cleveland, but no one knew of his record in Independence because he lied about his past employment.

But even if it had been another police officer, it may not have made a difference. A series of studies show that Black children are often viewed by white people to be up to four-and-a-half years older than they actually are.[2] This means that twelve-year-old Tamir Rice might have been perceived as nearly seventeen years old in the eyes of a white police officer. He would have been treated like an adult with a real gun (as he *was* treated) instead of a child with a toy gun (which he *actually* was).

1. Christine Mai-Duc, "Cleveland Officer Who Killed Tamir Rice Had Been Deemed Unfit for Duty," *Los Angeles Times*, posted December 3, 2014, https://www.latimes.com/nation/nationnow/la-na-nn-cleveland-tamir-rice-timothy-loehmann-20141203-story.html.
2. https://www.apa.org/news/press/releases/2014/03/black-boys-older.

Tamir wasn't even the first boy to die in this way. In 2007, twelve-year-old DeAntae Farrow was shot to death by a police officer in West Memphis, Arkansas, while he held a toy gun (although some eyewitnesses claim that DeAntae was only holding a soda pop and some chips). And, as in Tamir's case, no one was held responsible for DeAntae's murder. To many, Tamir's death brought up memories of a murder even farther back in time—the lynching of Emmett Till.

Time and again, unarmed Black women and men have died at the hands of those who have sworn to protect and serve them. It's not an issue of specific police officers or what their motivations are. The issue isn't racism in individuals; the issue is a system that again and again allows for racial injustice to occur.

Tamir Rice's death became a rallying cry for many to join the #BlackLivesMatter movement, which isn't trying to say that *only* Black lives matter but that Black lives matter too. Society has been set up so white lives have historically mattered more than those of people of color. The rules and laws in a society can lead to racial injustice even if individuals within that society do not intend for that to happen.

The ARC of Racial justice reminds us that just as individuals can act in racist ways, institutions can develop rules and practices that work against people of color. So what can we do to fix the system? How can we put new rules and practices in place that recognize God's image in everyone?

Questions to Consider

- What are some similarities between Tamir Rice and Emmett Till?
- How did the system fail Tamir Rice?

CHAPTER 22

Fighting Systemic Racism

When I went to college at the University of Notre Dame, Black people made up just 3 percent of the whole student body (that's compared to about a 13 percent average in the United States overall). For a long time I wondered why there were so few Black students at this amazing university. Then I learned that the university had recruiters and representatives who would travel to high schools to tell them about Notre Dame and get them to apply. No one from Notre Dame ever came to my high school. Most of the students at my high school were Black and Latinx kids. The schools the recruiters went to had mostly white students.

I'm sure the recruiters weren't intentionally trying to discriminate against Black and brown students, but their policy had been to go to only a select few schools to look for students. Because they recruited at places that did not have a lot of racial and ethnic minorities, they ended up with students mostly of the same race. This is a **systemic** problem. Systemic problems cannot be solved just by changing a person's attitudes; they can only be solved by changing the

Systemic: When racial inequities are built into the rules and exist apart from anyone's personal beliefs about other races and ethnicities

policies and practices of an organization. In this case, where and how the university recruits students has to change. In the same way, racism often functions within systems, not just in individuals, and the only way to fight these forms of racism is to change the rules and policies.

If the system has been set up to favor one group of people over another, we have to understand that a person's hardships aren't just a result of their actions. Some believe that people are poor because they are lazy. Others blame a person's circumstances, or matters beyond their control. In truth, both problems can affect poverty. But it is hardly fair when circumstances beyond a person's control make it so that no amount of effort can fix things. What is needed to fight against racism is to look at an individual's actions while also working to fix the problems in the system that keep those individuals down.

Remember the different prison sentences that were given to Jameel McGee (a Black man) and Andrew Collins (a white man) when they were arrested for having drugs? It did not matter that Jameel McGee was innocent of the crime and Andrew Collins was guilty. Jameel was sentenced to ten years in prison; Andrew was sentenced to eighteen months. The difference, according to the law, wasn't because of each man's race but the kind of drugs that were found at the scene. The drugs that Jameel was accused of having came with a five-year minimum prison sentence. Although Andrew had the same drugs, his were in a different form, which made it more expensive (thus less likely for Black people, who typically have less money than white people, to purchase and possess) and came with a much lower minimum prison sentence.

Fighting racism means looking at how people have set up the rules in society (like minimum prison sentences) and figuring out which ones are creating or keeping racial injustice as part of the system.

It Is About Impact, Not Intent

Have you ever seen an adult, like a bus driver, look over their shoulder to see out of the window before they switch lanes? They're not just checking to see if they passed a sign saying the McRib is back at McDonald's (yes, I'm one of those strange people who loves the McRib). They are looking to check their blind spot. As you can guess, a blind spot is an area where you can't see. Plenty of car accidents have been caused by people switching lanes without checking their blind spot. Did they *mean* to cause a car accident? Of course not. But a crash occurred and damage was done even if they didn't do it on purpose.

When it comes to racism, a lot of people will argue, "I didn't mean to be racist!" Instead of focusing on whether someone meant to be racist or not, we should pay more attention to the impact or outcome of their actions. It's the same with a rule or law. If a certain rule is used in a way that makes society less fair for people of color, then the rule itself might be racist even if it's not on purpose. The *intent* may have been okay, but the *impact* is racist. Racial justice advocates have to judge carefully both the intent and the impact of rules and practices.

One of the ways this plays out for kids is when schools have dress codes that unfairly target Black students. The hair of white people and Black people is different. In the United States, white hairstyles are considered normal, acceptable, and professional. Black hairstyles are often considered abnormal, unacceptable, and unprofessional. As a result, Black students are suspended twice as often as white students for dress code violations related to their hairstyles, with schools saying that the person's hair was too long, too different from their white classmates' hair, or simply not fitting with a teacher's preferred style. Such rules result in permanent marks on the student's record and make it more difficult for them to succeed later in life.

There's a Difference Between Guilt and Responsibility

Not long ago, I bought a used car. They are less expensive than new ones and still run pretty well. But they don't run perfectly. This car's air conditioner didn't work. At the time, I lived in the Mississippi Delta, where in the summertime you can start to sweat just walking from your house to the car in the driveway. The previous owner must have broken the air conditioner, but it was my problem now. In other words, I was not guilty of breaking the air conditioner, but now that the car was mine, I was responsible for fixing it.

People set up rules and laws a long time ago that still have an impact in the present. For instance, when Black people were denied loans to buy homes or pay for a college education, they lost the opportunity to build wealth (grow the amount of money they have) through homeownership or the higher-paying jobs that come with a college degree. Meanwhile, more white people had that opportunity and were able to build their wealth. To this day, white people have far more wealth than Black people, even though the specific laws have changed. What do we do about that?

Some will say, "Well, I didn't make the laws. I wasn't even alive back then. I shouldn't have to do anything." But there's a difference between guilt and responsibility. A person may not be guilty of a specific racist act, but in certain cases they may still be responsible. No one who reads this book has enslaved a Black person, but we are all still responsible for doing something about the harms that slavery caused. As we look at the laws and policies in society, we may not be guilty of creating them, but we are responsible for the world they created.

The next chapter looks at some ways we can go about putting our responsibility into action to make a difference.

Questions to Consider

- What are some rules you think are unfair? Why?
- Why aren't good intentions good enough?
- What is something you are responsible for fixing, even though you aren't guilty of breaking it?

CHAPTER 23

Racial Justice in Action: When to Speak Up

When you see an accident waiting to happen, you have to tell someone who can fix things. When your house is on fire, you have to shout out so other folks know to get out. When someone pronounces your name wrong, you have to politely set them straight, otherwise they'll keep pronouncing it incorrectly. There are times, big and small, when you have to speak up. Here are a few situations you're probably going to have to raise your voice in the fight against racism.

Interrupt Ignorance

Have you ever been in a group where someone is telling jokes? Maybe it starts out innocently enough. Like this one:

> A man is talking to God. "God, how long is a
>   million years?"
> God answers, "To me, it's about a minute."
> "God, how much is a million dollars?"
> "To me, it's a penny."

"God, may I have a penny?"
"Wait a minute."

But then the humor changes and someone tells a racist joke. Maybe they use a **racial slur**. Some people laugh. Others chuckle quietly and uncomfortably. Should you laugh along so you don't offend the joke-teller? Should you remain silent and forget about it? Should you call them out about the joke in front of people? What's the right thing to do?

> **Racial slur**: Offensive ways to refer to people from different racial or ethnic backgrounds than your own

You have to interrupt ignorance. *Ignorance* means someone doesn't know something. The joke-teller may not know that their humor is offensive (but sometimes they do and that's worse), but you still have to say something. It's important to speak up so the person knows you don't support the joke. Maybe it is best to talk to them one-on-one, but sometimes you might have to say that behavior is not okay in front of a group. The point is to explain to them why the joke was offensive—and don't let them shrug it off if they say they were only joking. Words are important, and they can be used as weapons to beat people up or as bandages to help people heal.

Be Willing to Admit When You Are Wrong

The Walt Disney Company is one of the largest businesses in the world. They own popular brands from Star Wars to Marvel and create entertainment content for people of all ages and interests. But Disney has had a troubled relationship with racial justice, specifically in the area of the historic use of racist stereotypes.

No company is perfect, and the larger a company is, the harder it is to get race right. But in the past few years, due to people speaking up about racism rather than staying silent, Disney was made aware of its mistakes and tried to make changes. To that end, Disney reached out to a group of experts to help them address the offensive content in their films. As a result, when you go to watch certain films available through the company's online platform (Disney+) you will see a twelve-second message, which cannot be skipped, telling viewers:

> This program includes negative depictions and/or mistreatment of people or cultures. These stereotypes were wrong then and are wrong now. Rather than remove this content, we want to acknowledge its harmful impact, learn from it and spark conversation to create a more inclusive future together.
>
> Disney is committed to creating stories with inspirational and aspirational themes that reflect the rich diversity of the human experience around the globe.
>
> To learn more about how stories have impacted society, please visit www.disney.com/StoriesMatter

The website referred to in the message above discusses the different ways racism played a role in the various Disney films that require the message to be shown.

Assembling a team of racial inclusivity experts and listening to what they have to say is part of making things right. Accepting responsibility for our past failures is a big part of working toward racial justice. And if the Walt Disney Company can start to acknowledge its failures and try to set things right, so can you.

Nobody is perfect when it comes to issues of race, but admitting and apologizing when you are wrong is a step in the right direction.

Go to Meetings

A lot of important decisions get made at meetings that seem boring. In high school, I always thought the themes for our dances were, well, unexciting—"Under the Sea" and "Oh, What a Night." Our student government chose the themes for each dance. I was a student representative for my class, but if they gave grades for participation in student government, I would have gotten an F.

I didn't go to many of the meetings. So when they decided on themes for dances and I didn't like them, I had no one to blame but myself.

Go to meetings like your student government meetings. Go to other meetings too, even the ones that seem really boring and made for adults. For instance, major decisions get made by your local school board. Ask your parents or guardians to take you to one just to see what it's like. Maybe you can get your teacher to give you extra credit for going if you write about the meeting. The point is that racism works through rules and policies, so get used to going to the meetings where those rules and policies are made.

Write a Letter to Your School Board

Believe it or not, many school systems are more segregated today than at almost any time in history. Although the Supreme Court ruled segregation illegal in 1954 with the *Brown v. Board of Education of Topeka* decision, the problem hasn't gone away. According to an article by the *New York Times*, "More than half of the nation's schoolchildren are in racially concentrated districts, where over 75 percent of students are either white or nonwhite."[1]

In many ways, people with money and racial privilege have sought to keep their schools separate from "those kids," which often refers to poor and working-class students and families of color. This has led to unequal funding and educational results between white students and students of color.

Public schools get their money through taxes (money paid to the government that goes toward certain programs and services). At the neighborhood level, a person's taxes are based on how much they could sell their house for. That means that poor neighborhoods have less money dedicated to their schools than wealthier neighborhoods. One report from 2016 revealed that school districts that mostly serve students of color received $23 billion less in funding than mostly white school districts, despite serving the same number of students. [2]

That may seem unfair to you, but what can you do? You're just a student, right? Actually, the decisions related to how school district lines are drawn happen at a very local level. You may even know the people responsible for drawing your school district. If you can't attend the meeting in person, talk to a teacher and find out if you can write to someone on the school board to encourage them to draw the lines so schools are less segregated. Better yet, see if your whole class or school

---

1. Sarah Mervosh, "How Much Wealthier Are White School Districts Than Nonwhite Ones? 23 Billion, Report Says," *New York Times*, February 27, 2019, www.nytimes .com/2019/02/27/education/school-districts-funding-white-minorities.html.
2. This report can be found at edbuild.org/content/23-billion#CA.

can send letters. As long as you're informed on the topic, a chorus of voices is louder than a solo. Your letter, when added to the others who also call for desegregation, can make a real difference to who attends your school.

You can also write your school board about dress code rules that may have racist roots as well as school suspension rates (to see if Black kids are suspended at a higher rate than white kids). You can encourage them to hire Black teachers, since the presence of a person of color in a role of authority can help all students succeed more equitably.

Your thoughts are important, and school boards need to hear that students like you care about racial justice.

Questions to Consider

- What would you say to someone who told a racist joke to you?
- Think of a time when you had to apologize for doing something mean. How did apologizing make things better?
- How do you think your school does in terms of racial justice?
- What will you say in your letter to the school board?

Ms. Fannie Lou's Fight

Although I grew up in the Midwest, I've spent my entire adult life in the Deep South, mainly in the Mississippi River Delta. I try not to draw stark lines between the South and other parts of the country because racism is not regional, but the South does stand out for its racial geography. Many of the Civil War's battles were fought there. The Civil Rights movement mainly happened in the South. These lands carry within them the voices of the ancestors.

One of my favorite of the many inspirational heroes to come from the South is Fannie Lou Hamer. To say that Ms. Hamer had a rough start to life is an understatement. She was born in 1917 as the twentieth and youngest child of Lou Ella and James Lee Townsend, and she started working in the cotton fields with her family at age six. By age twelve, she had to leave school to work in the fields full-time.

As if her life wasn't hard enough, Ms. Hamer, who came from a big family, had the ability to have babies stolen from her. One time she had to have a minor surgery. When she went into the operation, a white doctor, without her permission, removed the internal part of her body where babies grow. Some people wanted fewer Black people in the world, and removing their ability to have children was one way to make that happen. This horrible experience is one reason she got involved with the Civil Rights movement.

Fannie Lou Hamer went on to experience more hardship due to racism. On August 31, 1962, Ms. Hamer boarded a bus headed to the county seat with seventeen of her neighbors to register to vote. She and one other person were the only two allowed to fill out the voting application and take the required literacy test—a test that was designed to make Black people fail. No one was allowed to register to vote on that day.

Then on the ride home, Fannie Lou's bus was stopped by police and the driver was arrested. The charge? The bus was too yellow. While everyone was stuck on the bus, Fannie Lou began to sing. She sang "This Little Light of Mine," and soon the rest of the riders were singing with her.

> "This little light o' mine, I'm goin' let it shine
> Let it shine, let it shine, let it shine."

During another bus ride in 1963, Ms. Hamer was unjustly arrested. The bus she was on stopped off in Winona, Mississippi, for a break. Some of the activists she was with were refused service at a café. Shortly afterward, the police showed up to force Ms. Hamer's group to leave. When Fannie Lou Hamer asked the officer if they could continue on their way, she was arrested (even though that's what the police wanted her to do!).

Once Ms. Hamer and her fellow activists were in jail, they were all beaten. Fannie Lou was taken to a separate room, where the police ordered two prisoners to beat her severely. Ms. Hamer was almost killed in the attack and lived the rest of her days with a limp and a blood clot behind one of her eyes.

In spite of the cruel treatment she endured at the hands of the police, the fact that she lost her job on the plantation for attempting voter registration, and how she was insulted by the president of the United States (I wish we had time to get into all the details of her life!), Ms. Hamer continued to let her light shine for the rest of her life. She shed light on the racial injustices of her own voting experience, on the segregation built into Southern politics, and on school desegregation efforts. Her light inspired countless others to join in the fight against racism.

Fannie Lou Hamer started her life in poverty and had only the education provided to her by experience, but she became a beacon for the Civil Rights movement because of her passion and her faith. She oriented her life to racial justice, and so can you.

Fighting racism takes more than a few one-time actions. It is a lifetime of actions that happen naturally when you are turned toward racial justice. We have to turn ourselves spiritually, emotionally, culturally, and intellectually to see the many ways that racism affects life today.

When we are motivated by our love for God and for our neighbor and when we see how systems have been built to keep Black voices from being heard, we are ready to make a personal commitment toward racial justice.

Questions to Consider

- What stood out to you most about Fannie Lou Hamer's fight against racism?
- How might someone like Ms. Hamer encourage you to speak about racism?

CHAPTER 24

Orienting Your Life to Racial Justice

If racism happens when one group of people look down on another group because of their race or ethnicity, it is super important to make sure that you aren't guilty of the same kind of prideful outlook. It is way too easy, when you advocate for racial justice, to slip into a mindset of judgment on other people who aren't as active or as "woke" as you are. While you may have healthier beliefs about race and a deeper understanding of how things got this way, you do not have the right to disrespect other people.

When someone you know starts spouting racist things or shows they don't understand the true nature of racism, you may be tempted to roll your eyes, use sarcasm, or mock them. Remember that at one time you might have done the same thing. Remember that they are made in the image of God too. Be humble.

Philippians 2:3–4 says, "Do nothing out of selfish ambition or vain conceit. Rather, in humility value others above yourselves, not looking to your own interests but each of you to the interests of the others." This is the mindset we must have as we pursue racial justice as a way of life. Fighting racism is ultimately about serving others from a wellspring of love.

To pursue racial justice, we must grow in humility—listening and learning, yes, but also admitting that we, too, can act in racist ways. We must have the humility to realize how we have benefitted from the racial status quo. White people must recognize with humility that, although life can be difficult for anyone, their skin color hasn't added to their hardships. People of color must recognize that, despite their life experiences, they can sometimes get it wrong when it comes to race.

In Matthew 7, Jesus confronts those who would hold themselves up as good examples and judge others while ignoring the ways they are flawed. "Why do you look at the speck of sawdust in your brother's eye and pay no attention to the plank in your own eye?" (Matt. 7:3). In our journey toward racial justice, we must always be aware of the ways we may encourage racism, even if unintentionally, and seek to correct our attitudes and behaviors. To be useful in helping others fight racism, we need to correct it in our own lives first. As Jesus put it, "You hypocrite, first take the plank out of your own eye, and then you will see clearly to remove the speck from your brother's eye" (Matt. 7:5).

This can be especially difficult for white people, to whom racism is designed to be invisible. When a white person is made aware of the reality of racism, it can make them feel attacked. There's no way around this feeling, but having humility can make the process of learning and growing much faster and easier.

For people of any race or ethnicity, humility is a key attitude in the work of racial justice. It takes humble honesty to consider one's shortcomings and still pursue the work of fighting racism. Humility allows new information to correct old ideas and leads us into better ways of loving one another.

Keep the Light Switch On

There's a big difference between a light switch and a smoke alarm. A light switch can be turned on and off. A smoke alarm is always on. Racial justice for white people is often like a light switch. You can turn it on or off whenever you feel like it. But for people of color, racial justice is more like a smoke alarm. It always has to be on just to keep safe and avoid danger.

Every day, people of color in the United States are reminded that they are different or "other." They are reminded of their less-than status when they are followed around by employees or security guards in stores, when someone tries to pronounce their name, when they are zoned to attend a particular school, when they receive a paycheck with a lower amount than their white coworker, when they see another instance of police brutality used against someone who looks like them. By contrast, white people may never think about themselves or their neighbors in racial terms. What happens or does not happen to them seems to be up to chance and personal decisions. Race may hardly seem like a factor at all.

Since race affects white people and people of color so differently, one of the most important racial justice practices is to keep race at the top of your mind even when you have the option of not doing so. For white people, this shows people of color that someone has their back in the fight against racism. To tune in to racial issues for a little while and then go back to life as usual whenever it is convenient doesn't say much for someone's commitment. Racial justice is demonstrated not in the times when everyone is talking about race but in those times when it would be easy or expected to overlook race.

The only way to keep the racial justice light switch on is to set up a plan. Don't rely on willpower alone. Your plan for racial justice could include group participation—reading books with others, seeking out interracial friendships, or getting involved with an organization where racial justice is a priority. However you choose to do it, don't allow your light switch to turn off.

> *"This little light o' mine, I'm goin' let it shine*
> *Let it shine, let it shine, let it shine."*

Questions to Consider

- Why is humility necessary to pursue racial justice?
- How could you make sure there isn't a "plank" in your own eye before trying to remove a "speck" from your brother's or sister's eye?
- Why is racial justice like a light switch for most white people? How can you make sure your light stays on?

CHAPTER 25

Racial Justice in Action: Use Your Voice

F annie Lou Hamer showed her commitment to racial justice, not just by facing threats head-on but by setting aside time for traveling, speaking, and encouraging others to register to vote. How will you turn your commitment into a lifelong pursuit? It starts with making time and using your voice.

Make Time for Racial Justice

The reasons more people don't fight for racial justice can be deep and complicated, but sometimes they're pretty simple. To practice racial justice, you must make time for it. It takes time to ask questions, to read books, to write letters, and to do all the tasks necessary for a life of racial justice activism. And you are likely busy with sports and homework and chores and being a kid. So the idea of setting aside time for racial justice may seem overwhelming, but that's what must be done.

Getting serious about fighting racism means paying attention to how you spend your time. It means being willing to put down some things you like for other things you know are important.

A good first step is to keep a time journal for a week to see what kind of time you have available. On a piece of paper or in a notebook, jot down where your time goes. Make a note every time you switch activities and write down what time it is. Just being aware of how you spend your time helps you use it more wisely.

You can even make fighting racism part of your homework. *Groan!* I know, I know. But think of homework as practice. If you spend time on racial justice at home, just like a school homework assignment, then you are practicing and getting better at fighting racism.

Once you have an idea of how much time you can give to racial justice causes, be intentional about doing so. And remember, it isn't always a matter of marching like Audrey Faye Hendricks or speaking up like Rosa Parks. The time you spend thinking, praying, and planning is time that counts toward fighting racism too.

> **The time you spend thinking, praying, and planning is time that counts toward fighting racism too.**

See Something, Say Something

Everyone has a voice. Some people, like Barack Obama and Kamala Harris, have voices that carry farther because of where they stand. Others, like Emmett Till and Tamir Rice, have voices that are heard because they were silenced too soon. Whether your voice is used to address a march on Washington D.C. like Martin Luther King Jr. or simply to speak up when someone tells a racist joke, everyone has a voice.

What are the best ways for you to use yours? Here are three situations where you should speak up. First, if someone is acting in racist ways to you (using racial slurs, name-calling, or treating you differently because of your skin color or ethnicity), you have the right to say something. Talk to your parents, find a trustworthy adult, maybe a youth leader or pastor. No one has the right to make less of you. You bear the image of God, and to treat you poorly is an offense against God.

Second, use your voice when you see an issue that directly affects your community. If someone in your family, school, church, or town is experiencing racism, your voice is needed to make sure people know what you believe and with whom you stand.

Third, if someone who claims to be fighting racism alongside you does something you know is wrong, go to them and talk about it. If it isn't someone you know personally, consider ways you can let others know that you don't share that person's views and you don't agree with how they act.

In each situation, be prepared for some kind of reaction. Not everyone will agree with you. Some people won't understand your stand against racism. They may think you are making a big deal over nothing. Others will want to argue with you. But some people will agree with you and encourage you. The benefit of speaking up for racial justice is that people of color will feel seen and heard. No matter how many negative responses you get, speaking up to promote racial justice is the right thing to do.

Questions to Consider

- How do you spend your free time? How can you use more of it for racial justice?
- Have you ever spoken up about something that was wrong (like racism!)? How did it make you feel? Would you do it again?

Your Fight

This book begins with the question, "Can kids actually fight against racism?" The answer, in case you still don't know, is yes.

You can fight it by being aware of its existence, by recognizing the different ways it has played out throughout history, and by understanding how you have been affected by it. You can fight it by pursuing relationships with people from different backgrounds than your own, by seeking to be a good friend, and by seeing God's image in everyone. You can fight it by committing to set right the wrongs of the past, by accepting responsibility when others say it isn't your job, and by keeping your light switch flipped on. Use the ARC of Racial Justice as a model to help you remember the different ways you can fight racism.

> Use the ARC of Racial Justice as a model to help you remember the different ways you can fight racism.

Maybe this book has opened your eyes to the reality of racism and you are a little unsure if you even want to join the fight. After all, people have been hurt and killed for protesting against racism throughout the history of this nation. How will you know you won't suffer the same way? Isn't that a bit much to be asking of a young person . . . or anyone?

It's true. When I began intentionally dedicating my time, expertise, and energy to fighting racism, my life did not get easier. In many ways it became harder. I opened myself up to arguments and attacks. Relationships became strained and some were broken. In paying closer attention to racial injustice, I felt the pain of it more deeply.

And yes, getting involved in the fight against racism is a lot to ask of a person, especially a kid. Some people think kids should be free to live in happy ignorance of the ways this world is broken. But I think some people underestimate kids and how much they understand. You already know the world is broken. You hear it when your parents talk to each other about the news. You see it in how kids treat each other and make fun of each other. So I think you would be happier being part of making things better instead of pretending they are already good.

Besides, there are definite upsides to taking on this fight. My journey of racial justice has brought me a deeper sense of three realities: God's presence, the community of my fellow fighters, and my identity.

In the times when I have felt the most burdened by the brokenness of the world, Christ has come alongside me and helped me feel whole in him. And although my fight for racial justice has made some people distance themselves from me, it has brought me into a community with many others.

Fighting for racial justice has taught me more about . . . me. I am far more fragile than I like to admit. I make the same mistakes that I tell others to avoid. I get tired, frustrated, angry. I have also discovered reservoirs of previously untapped resilience. I am learning to ask for help when I need it. I have learned lessons from others about how to be broken by injustice and still have joy at the same time.

This can be true for you too. Your age doesn't make a difference. We are in this together. We cannot give up. We are people of hope. We are people who believe that a poor carpenter from Nazareth conquered death and is forming a people who will join in his victory. Each day that we live is the opportunity to bear witness to the resurrection life and the coming of the kingdom of God. We pray and work for that kingdom to come and for God's will to be done, not just later but right here and now.

We are in the Civil Rights movement of our day. One day people will be writing books about this time in history. Maybe your story of fighting racism will be part of what they remember. You can be an example to other people around you and even people who live long after you. Tomorrow is too late to get started fighting racism. Today is the day and now is the time to join the journey toward racial justice.

Glossary

Abolition: The end of slavery

Activist: A person who is actively committed to changing society to become more just

Anti-Black police brutality: Police methods that treat Black people in more forceful, and sometimes dangerous, ways than how they treat white people

Appropriate: Take something for one's own use, usually without the owner's permission

Bias: A tendency to be for or against something based on personal judgment instead of facts

Black Power movement: A historical period in the 1960s and 1970s when people promoted the idea that Black people should be able to lead their own communities by electing officials, owning businesses, fostering a positive sense of self, and resisting racism

Boycott: Agree as a community not to buy or use services from a specific business as a form of protest against the business's unfair rules or policies

Desegregate: To remove the rules that keep white people and Black people apart so everyone can have equal access to the same resources

Discriminate: To treat people differently based on characteristics such as how they look, where they're from, or what they believe

Displacement: The forced relocation of people to another part of the country

Emancipation: Being set free

Equity: Giving everyone what they need to succeed, even if what they need is different from what others need

Indigenous people: The earliest known people to live in a specific region

Ku Klux Klan: A white supremacist group that was popular after slavery ended and opposed, sometimes violently, Black people getting their full civil rights

Law-and-order politics: A strategy where politicians promise to be tough on crime in the name of protecting citizens, which can result in brutal policing tactics and unfair prison sentences for minor crimes

Lynching: A form of terrorism where groups of white people kill Black people who have been accused of a crime but haven't been given a fair trial in court

Mass incarceration: Locking up a large population of people

Melanin: The pigment that gives skin and hair its color

Nationalism: The belief that the country where you live is the best country in the world and that people coming in from other countries will make things worse in some way

Plantation: A large area of farmland that was owned by a wealthy person who relied on the labor of poorer people, typically enslaved Black people, to plant and harvest crops

Prejudice: An opinion, usually negative, about someone else that isn't based on truth

Race-based chattel slavery: The practice of owning Black people for their labor and treating them as though they were property that could be bought and sold and used like an object

Racial profiling: Paying closer attention to Black people and people of color because you suspect them of illegal activity based on the color of their skin alone

Racial slur: Offensive ways to refer to people from different racial or ethnic backgrounds than your own

Segregation: A system of keeping Black people and other people of color separated from white people

Slave patrols: Groups of armed white men who policed enslaved Black people and who captured Black people who escaped slavery

Systemic: When racial inequities are built into the rules and exist apart from anyone's personal beliefs about other races and ethnicities

White supremacy: A system of power where language, lifestyles, and values held by white people are considered normal and better than those held by people of color

Appendix

A Word About Hair

For some reason, white people are often tempted to touch Black people's hair, and some Black people are tempted to touch white people's hair.

It could be curiosity. *What does it feel like? It's so different from my own hair. How do you wash it and style it?* Being curious about differences is a good thing, but if curiosity leads to touching, it's not okay.

No one has the right to touch your body without your permission. For Black people especially, getting unwanted touches from white people sends a message that white people feel like they should be allowed to use a Black person's body as they see fit. It's a reminder of slavery, when white people could do whatever they wanted with a Black person's body because enslaved people were considered property.

The other problem with focusing on how different a person's hair is, is that it can make that person feel different in other ways. If their hair is unique, your interest and curiosity might feel to them like you are saying that they don't fit in with everyone else. Even complimenting someone on the thing that makes them different can make them feel different and unwelcome. The best thing to do is recognize the differences between you without using them to make someone feel singled out.

How Do I Handle . . .

. . . when someone I love is saying hurtful things about other races?

We all want to believe the people we love—our parents, grandparents, other family members, and friends—make good choices most of the time. So when one of those people says something you know to be hurtful and wrong, it can be more than a little upsetting. It can feel like you don't really know this person like you thought you did. Whether someone is telling racist jokes, using racial slurs, or reinforcing offensive stereotypes, it is never okay to speak in racist ways. At the same time, you love this person. What's the deal?

Some people may think racism is okay when they think it's funny or if the people they are speaking to fall into the same ethnic category. Some may not even know they are being hurtful with their words because they grew up thinking these things are acceptable. In either case, it is a good idea to talk to the speaker when it is just you and them, especially if they are older than you. Respect your elders even as you try to point out why they are wrong.

When you have their attention, say something like, "You know I love you, but I'm having a hard time with something you said earlier." Then you can tell them what the offensive thing was and why you thought it was offensive. For people who say hurtful things because they don't know any better, this is an opportunity to teach them something new. For those who know exactly what they are saying, they may not listen, but you'll have shown them that you think fighting racism is important.

The important thing about the conversation is to speak with love. Be curious. You might ask what resources, news stations, books, articles, or experiences make them say or believe what they do. But don't back down if what they say is harmful or wrong. Our words matter. The Bible says so (see Proverbs 21:23, Ephesians 4:29, and James 1:26).

If what the person said really made you angry, you may need to give it some time before you are ready to speak with love. Talk with someone else and get another perspective. Pray about the situation. Pray that the person will listen to you. Pray that God will help you speak up. Philippians 4:6 says, "Do not be anxious about anything, but in every situation, by prayer and petition, with thanksgiving, present your requests to God."

. . . when someone says something racist to me?

Being called a racial slur is a shock, no matter how often it happens in the world. To be denied your worth as a human being made in God's image is wrong, and your body may react like it isn't just an insult but a serious threat. Before you run away or punch someone, take a second to breathe and pray.

Pausing to pray does a couple things. First, it makes sure that you don't react poorly to the offense. Second, it gets your mind aligned with God's so you can see them as a sinner in need of grace (just like you are).

Next, if the incident happened at school or church, tell a school employee or church leader what happened. Although we live in a broken world where incidents like this still happen, we live in a different world than the one fifty years ago where these incidents were actively ignored. Racist slurs and threats are serious matters that schools need to take seriously. The consequences for the person who used them will likely be more severe than you could make happen on your own. If other people heard the situation, ask them to come with you while you make your report to the school, so they can have other eyewitnesses to support what happened.

If the incident didn't happen around other people, walking away may be your best way forward. Don't give in to the temptation to physically fight them. If no one else was around when it happened, be sure to tell your family or other trusted adults about the incident as soon as you can and let them help you decide how to deal with the situation.

. . . when others disagree with my stand for racial justice?

Everyone knows someone who is a "racial justice resister." These are folks who may claim not to have a "racist bone" in their body, but they don't believe that racism is still a problem in today's society, so they aren't doing anything to fight against it.

It may seem like these people put on blindfolds so they don't see the racism that happens around them. Facts and figures about the reality of racism do little to convince these folks, so how can you get through?

First, ask yourself if the topic is worth talking about. How well do you know the other person? If it's someone you know well and see all the time, you'll have better luck in having a conversation than if the person is someone you just met, or barely talk to, or who you only know through social media.

Second, talk to them without looking down on them.

Show the person who disagrees with you the kind of respect you are hoping to get back from them. If you are hoping that they'll see your point—that everyone is made in God's image and worthy to be treated well—you have to start by treating them well. Showing respect is a great way to get someone to listen to you.

Third, you can ask them to trade books with you. They might not think racism is a big deal because of something they read or heard about. Offer to read one of their books if they'll agree to read a book that helped you decide to get active in the fight against racism (maybe this one!).

When a person is willing to listen to why you see things the way you do, you can introduce them to the facts around historical racism and the need to set things right. But while these facts may help break down walls in a person's head, the root of resistance to racial justice is found in the heart. This comes through prayer and patience. After all, the fight against racism is not against people who deny its reality but against powers far worse (check out Ephesians 6:12).

Some Books to Read About Race

The best books in the world act as windows into the lives of others and mirrors into our own. The books listed below offer a mix of both. Reading books by diverse authors and about diverse characters can help us see things from a different point of view, but they'll also show us how we can relate to the struggles and emotions in very personal ways. Some of these books may have language typical from the era and situation they are set in, but it is important to know that they represent the reality of life, even if they are fictional stories.

The Watsons Go to Birmingham—1963 by Christopher Paul Curtis

Ghost Boys by Jewell Parker Rhodes

Lizzie Bright and the Buckminster Boy by Gary D. Schmidt

Betty Before X by Ilyasah Shabazz and Renee Watson

New Kid by Jerry Craft

One Crazy Summer by Rita Williams-Garcia

Juneteenth Jamboree by Carole Boston Weatherford and Yvonne Buchanan

All Different Now by Angela Johnson and E.B. Lewis

Opal Lee and What It Means to Be Free by Alice Faye Duncan and Keturah A. Bobo

March Graphic Novel Trilogy by John Lewis, Andrew Aydin, and Nate Powell

Genesis Begins Again by Alicia D. Williams

The Track Series by Jason Reynolds

The Hate U Give by Angie Thomas

Stamped by Ibram X. Kendi and Jason Reynolds

Additional Articles

What Is White Supremacy?

White supremacy is the belief or assumption that white people and their culture are naturally superior to other people and cultures. While I often use the term *racism*, white supremacy includes racism of all kinds that gives social, cultural, and political advantages to those seen as white. If we want to fight racism, we must fight white supremacy as well. White supremacy is the reason that white people bear so much responsibility in the fight against racism.

What Is Affirmative Action?

Affirmative action refers to taking steps *on purpose* toward intentionally welcoming into a community people who have been historically excluded from that community. If a people or an organization has excluded people on purpose, then they must also include people on purpose. Affirmative action means putting a plan into action to include people of color on purpose. It is a way to make right past wrongs and to give a fighting chance to people who had no chance to succeed in the past.

In the words of Martin Luther King Jr., "A society that has done something special *against* the Negro for hundreds of years must now do something special *for* him, in order to equip him to compete on an equal basis."[1]

Some people may think that focusing on race and ethnicity when putting together a community sounds like a kind of "reverse racism," but ignoring race leads to a "colorblind" problem. What does that mean? It means that if society has been set up to favor white people over Black people, ignoring race—being colorblind—will mean society will continue to favor white people over Black people. Affirmative action is a plan to give equal chances to people who have been treated unequally in society.

What Is White Privilege?

Just like racism makes life harder for Black people and other people of color, racism actually can make life easier in some ways for white people. Racism was designed to benefit a certain group of people—in this case, white people. The benefits white people receive in a racist society are sometimes referred to as white privilege.

White privilege takes many forms:

- White people usually do not get followed around in stores simply because of the color of their skin.
- If you have a name like Emily or Greg, which are perceived as "white-sounding" names, then you are more likely to get a job than someone named Lakisha or Jamal, which are perceived as "Black-sounding" names.

---

1. Martin Luther King Jr., *Where Do We Go from Here: Chaos or Community?* (Boston, MA: Beacon, 1967), 95.

- If you are white, you have a better chance of getting a loan from the bank, owning a home, and even living longer.

White privilege does not mean that life is easy for all white people. It just means that your skin color is not an obstacle to achieving your goals.

It also means that a white person's experiences are considered normal, and the lives of people of color are considered to be exotic. It can mean that bandages are made to blend in with white skin instead of Black skin, or that it is more difficult to find books, movies, and TV shows featuring people who look like you.

And the sneaky thing about white privilege is that it is practically invisible to most white people. It's like trying to explain water to a fish. It's just the thing they live in and they're so used to it that they don't even think about it. Many white people don't think to look at the differences between themselves and people of color. Recognizing the presence of white privilege in society is an important step toward fighting racism, especially when it tries to be invisible.

The Myth of the Model Minority

Racial and ethnic minorities are groups of people that are smaller than the majority group in terms of numbers, so in the United States, for now, the majority is currently made up of white people. Every group of people looks, sounds, and acts differently, but the majority or dominant group often looks at the differences of those in the minority as threatening, dangerous, or just plain weird. Instead of embracing these differences as being designed to show God's creativity, white people want racial and ethnic minorities to act more like white people and reflect the values they hold to be most important. That's where the "model minority" comes from. A model minority member is the "perfect" kind of immigrant or person of color who only gets good grades and has a professional job like a doctor or lawyer. This is unfair because it forces immigrants and people of color into a one-size-fits all mold of "success." It denies the problems and challenges they face due to their race or nation of origin. And the dominant group uses the model minority myth against other people of color by saying, "See how well this other group is doing? Why can't you be more like them?"

A Parent's Guide to Helping Your Kids Fight Racism

The best time to talk to kids about race is early and often. This book is aimed at kids between the ages of eight and twelve, and these years are crucial in forming healthy outlooks on race. This age is when kids start making their own judgments. This is when they start asking why the world is the way it is.

If we don't address racism with our young people, they will get their information from other sources. My hope is that through this book, you as a parent, guardian, or trusted adult will be able to help the kids in your life understand an important part of their identity.

The best time to talk to kids about race is early and often.

You'll be able to help them embrace what it means to be made in God's image and to help them see others in the same light. But it is hard to teach what you do not know, and kids have lots of questions.

The first step in teaching kids about race is teaching yourself. You cannot appropriately respond to someone else's questions about race if you have not asked and attempted to answer your own. The more you increase your capacity around issues of race and racism, the better you will be able to teach young people about the topic.

Teaching kids about race is similar in some ways to teaching kids about sex. Sex and sexuality are delicate topics that are personal and fraught with confusion and the potential for harm. At the same time, they are far too important not to discuss. If adults avoid teaching kids sexual ethics, then kids will likely get their information from potentially less helpful sources such as pop culture or their peers. The same is true regarding racial justice. It is incumbent on the adults who care about children to make sure they know as much as possible about how to be a gracious and compassionate adult, especially on the topic of race.

When talking to kids about race, it is often necessary to push through your fears. *What if I say the wrong thing? What if I don't know the answer? What if I am replicating the racism I've seen or grown up with?* These questions are natural and unavoidable. You cannot go around them; you must push through them. Bumbling through a conversation about race is often better than not having a conversation at all, and the more you do it, the better you'll get.

You must also realize that talking about race is not a one-time lecture but an ongoing dialogue. You cannot sit down and have *the* "race talk" with kids; you must have many "race talks." Knowing that you have multiple opportunities to talk to kids about race should also relieve some of the pressure. You do not need to cram every bit of necessary information into a single conversation. And if you happen to get something wrong or you later realize how you could have explained something better, don't worry; you may have the opportunity to revisit the dialogue at a later point.

You can always pull out this book again and cover a topic as situations arise. Every conversation about race will make the next conversation less awkward to have. And connecting abstract conversations about race to the real world—memories, trips they've taken, books they've read, current events—is usually a good practice.

But we can't just talk to kids about race; we have to show them about race too. When learning how to multiply in grade school, you may remember your teacher pulling out base ten blocks. They were little cubes arranged in rows of ones, tens, or hundreds designed to make the abstract principle of multiplication understandable through the use of tangible objects. In a similar way, a child learning about race may find the concept confusing when it is only described using words. Adults can help children understand race, and more importantly racial justice, by using concrete examples and experiences.

Visuals can help a child better understand race. Going to the physical site of a place that has an important story to tell about racial justice or injustice can help. You can read historical markers aloud, walk around the building or the location, learn about the place online beforehand, and use the entire experience as a conversation catalyst.

The best conversations about race intersect organically with what children experience regularly in their world. Whether it comes from a comment a cartoon character made or an interaction at the grocery store, pausing in the moment or soon thereafter to talk about race makes such conversations feel normal and regular.[1] Using the culture, spaces, and relationships

---

1. The Disney film *Zootopia*, for instance, presents ample opportunities to discuss differences, prejudice, and reconciliation in the context of an animated movie that uses different animals in ways analogous to different people groups in the real world.